FTCE

Music
Practice Questions

I0879916

Mometrix
TEST PREPARATION

Dear Future Exam Success Story

First of all, **THANK YOU** for purchasing Mometrix study materials!

Second, congratulations! You are one of the few determined test-takers who are committed to doing whatever it takes to excel on your exam. **You have come to the right place.** We developed these practice tests with one goal in mind: to deliver you the best possible approximation of the questions you will see on test day.

Standardized testing is one of the biggest obstacles on your road to success, which only increases the importance of doing well in the high-pressure, high-stakes environment of test day. Your results on this test could have a significant impact on your future, and these practice tests will give you the repetitions you need to build your familiarity and confidence with the test content and format to help you achieve your full potential on test day.

Your success is our success

We would love to hear from you! If you would like to share the story of your exam success or if you have any questions or comments in regard to our products, please contact us at **800-673-8175** or **support@mometrix.com**.

Thanks again for your business and we wish you continued success!

Sincerely,
The Mometrix Test Preparation Team

Printed in the United States of America

Table of Contents

Practice Test #1

1. What is NOT an aspect of the score the conductor needs to learn when preparing a score?

a. Form
b. Transpositions
c. Publisher
d. Dynamics

2. Which of the following initial techniques used to teach students to sing harmony is most appropriate?

a. Singing root harmonies
b. Singing in thirds
c. Singing drones in fifths
d. Experimenting to find harmony while someone else sings melody

3. A loud, forceful, and fast sound tends to convey which of the following moods?

a. Sorrow
b. Calm
c. Hope
d. Passion

4. Which of the following differentiated instructional strategies is most practical when teaching guitar in a general music setting?

a. Separate high achievers from low achievers.
b. Eliminate individual formative assessments.
c. Provide each student with short personal lessons.
d. Design group projects based upon mutual interests.

5. Which of the following interval pattern sequences does Kodály advocate teaching students to sing?

a. *So-mi, so-mi-la*
b. *So-mi, mi-re-do*
c. *Mi-re-do, fa-ti*
d. *Mi-re-do, so-mi-la*

6. Which of the following concert preparations for an upcoming school year is the first behavior that a music teacher should engage in?

a. Choosing dates for concerts
b. Signing out facilities
c. Preparing a checklist
d. Informing stakeholders of plans

7. Of the commonly accepted and understood time periods into which Western classical music has been divided, which period is associated most strongly with musical nationalism?

a. Baroque
b. Classical
c. Romantic
d. Contemporary

8. For beginning clarinet players, which of the following pitches are best used in sequence to help the player tune the instrument to itself and then to an ensemble?

a. E3, G5
b. G4, G3
c. C4, C5
d. G3, E4

9. Which trumpet mute, also known by the brand name Harmon mute, produces a buzzed tone and is often associated with Miles Davis during his cool jazz period?

a. Straight mute
b. Wah-wah mute
c. Cup mute
d. Bucket mute

10. What is the name of the note below?

a. Hemidemisemiquaver
b. Demisemiquaver
c. Semiquaver
d. Quaver

11. Which of the physical aspects of brass performance directly affects changes in dynamics?

a. Embouchure
b. Frequency
c. Posture
d. Volume of air

12. Which of the following physical actions performed on a student best legally defines "physical restraint"?

a. Personal restriction that prevents a student from moving
b. Physical escort to a school safety officer or front office
c. The use of any device to restrict a student's mobility
d. Vehicle safety apparatus used to transport a student

13. Of the following Cuban styles, which is derived from the mambo with a characteristic rhythmic pattern of two eighth notes followed by a quarter note?

a. Tresillo
b. Cha-cha-cha
c. Son montuno
d. Rumba

14. Which of the following statements about the music achievement potential of an individual with a disability is most appropriate to consider in teaching and learning music?

a. Cognitively impaired students generally prefer dancing/singing to playing an instrument.
b. It is generally harder for a student with cognitive impairment to learn how to sing in tune.
c. IQ is a weak predictor of music aptitude and the potential to achieve in music.
d. A student with low music achievement will also have low music aptitude.

15. Which of the following is generally considered an advantage of a mixer over an audio interface for a recording studio?

a. Greater portability
b. Less expensive
c. Overall simpler to use
d. More control of sound

16. When encountering a difficult passage, how do musicians most effectively practice that passage?

a. Playing it as fast as possible
b. Studying it away from the instrument
c. Playing it slowly and thoughtfully
d. Playing the sections before and after

17. Compared to a condenser microphone, which of the following reasons is the best for choosing a dynamic microphone?

a. Greater sensitivity and output
b. No need for phantom power
c. Better suited for the studio
d. Better suited for higher frequencies

18. When a music teacher works with young, beginning instrumentalists by having them focus on hearing and internalizing music (audiation) through listening activities and playing music by ear before being introduced to music notation, they are following the learning theory of which music educator?

a. Suzuki
b. Gordon
c. Dalcroze
d. Kodály

19. Which of the following keys is a standard English horn pitched in?

a. Concert C
b. Concert F
c. Concert Eb
d. Concert Bb

20. The sound wave frequency of a musical note is its:

a. Tempo
b. Melody
c. Pitch
d. Rhythm

21. A student choral committee is planning a year-end banquet and wants to create a video montage of graduating seniors throughout the year. Which of the following types of copyright license will allow the committee to use copyrighted music performances to play over the video?

a. Grand license
b. Mechanical license
c. Compulsory license
d. Synchronization license

22. The overtone series can be best understood within the context of which scientific discipline?

a. Chemistry
b. Biology
c. Physics
d. Astronomy

23. Which movement of the 19th century featured music that evoked a place through the use of folk melodies?

a. Impressionism
b. Nationalism
c. Romanticism
d. Realism

24. When teaching a rote song, which of the following is the primary justification for the teacher using the technique of singing the song or performing an instrumental version for students while asking them to do several activities, such as raising a hand every time a specific word is sung, identifying repeating patterns, or saying what the first and last words of the song are?

a. Promotes the creation of a gestalt during learning
b. Provides opportunities for teacher modeling
c. Efficiently and enjoyably teaches by rote
d. Students learn without realizing they are learning

25. In standard twelve-bar blues form, where would one expect to find the "turnaround"?

a. the first bar
b. the fourth bar
c. the eighth bar
d. the twelfth bar

26. Who of the following is credited with composing the following Requiem excerpt?

a. Wolfgang Mozart
b. Luigi Cherubini
c. Michael Haydn
d. Hector Berlioz

27. Which of the following regions of the world does the gamelan come from?

a. Pakistan
b. Indonesia
c. China
d. Australia

28. Which of the following statements is true of vocal changes in developing adolescents?

a. It is largely a myth and can be kept in check by teaching proper technique.
b. Girls' singing voices do not change, although boys' singing voices do change.
c. Because their voices change in unpredictable ways, boys should stop singing during the middle school years and then resume in high school.
d. Girls' singing voices change just as boys' voices do.

29. Which music era is the following music excerpt likely from?

a. Baroque
b. Classical
c. Romantic
d. Neoclassical

30. Which of the following fundamental embouchure characteristics applies to all brass instruments?

a. The tongue says "eeh," and the corners of the lips are pulled back.
b. The tongue is pointed, and the center of the lips is pursed.
c. The corners of the lips are tight and pulled back with a flat chin.
d. The cheeks are puffed, and the chin is rounded.

31. Which of the following instructional planning techniques is most associated with evidence-centered design (ECD)?

a. Write unit goals
b. Use backwards mapping
c. Plan learning experiences first
d. Align with national and state standards

32. How should a conductor's elbow generally be positioned?

a. Raised high above the podium
b. Close to the torso
c. Pointed to the front of the ensemble
d. Slightly raised away from the body

33. Why might a progressive music teacher who emphasizes solfege advocate for a beginning baritone student to learn to read both treble and bass clef simultaneously?

a. If a student is proficient in interpreting solfege, transposing between the two clefs becomes fairly easy.
b. Beginning music for the baritone is written in treble clef.
c. Baritone players often switch from playing trumpet.
d. Using treble clef eliminates the use of ledger lines.

34. Which of the following should be done first when harmonizing a given melody?

a. Execution
b. Planning
c. Testing
d. Analysis

35. When working with ensembles to achieve an appropriate ensemble sound, which of the following sequences of conceptual sonic factors is most appropriate to teach?

a. Balance, blend, intonation, characteristic sound
b. Blend, balance, intonation, characteristic sound
c. Blend, balance, characteristic sound, intonation
d. Characteristic sound, intonation, blend, balance

36. When using a standard trigger on a Bb tenor trombone, which of the following intervals does the trigger expand the instrument's range by?

a. Lowers by a perfect fourth
b. Lowers by a perfect fifth
c. Raises by a major third
d. Raises by a perfect fifth

37. Compared to the Classical era, which of the following stylistic characteristics of this music excerpt best exemplifies that it was composed during the Baroque era?

(Bach's Keyboard Sonata in D minor BWV 964)

a. Basso continuo
b. Polyphonic texture
c. Continuous motion
d. Symmetrical melody

38. Which of the following subtests from the Iowa Tests of Music Literacy (ITML) achievement battery requires students to indicate the chord progressions that they are listening to?

a. Tonal audiation/listening
b. Tonal audiation/reading
c. Tonal audiation/writing
d. Tonal audiation/improvising

39. Which of the following factors related to teaching to individual differences is most evident in the rating scale illustrated below?

Q&A Antecedent and Consequent Phrases Improvisation Rating Scale

1. Student responds, but the response is completely unmusical.
2. Student performs a song and a sense of melodic contour is evident. Student sings resting tone in tune. Does not demonstrate a sense of tonal syntax.
3. Student sings the resting tone and some pitches in tune, but does not sing tonal functions (e.g., V-I/IV-I or diatonic) that act as cadences in consequent phrases. Student demonstrates some sense of tonal syntax.
4. Student sings resting tone and some pitches in tune. Student sings a tonal function that can be included in a consequent phrase. Student demonstrates a sense of tonal syntax.
5. Student sings resting tone in tune and sings most tonal functions and pitches associated with a consequent phrase in tune. Student demonstrates a clear sense of tonal syntax by locking in tonality.
6. Student begins and ends in tune. Student sings all tonal functions and pitches associated with a consequent phrase in tune. Student demonstrates a clear sense of tonal syntax.

a. It is based upon the student responding with a consequent phrase.
b. It is a single-dimensional continuous rating scale.
c. The criteria within the rating scale are subjective.
d. Most students will score neither a 1 nor a 6.

40. Students pretend to pick up and drink a teacup filled with tea. Then, students pretend to pick up a teacup filled with liquid lead. Which of Laban's effort elements are most directly changed?

a. Weight and flow
b. Time and space
c. Weight and space
d. Time and flow

41. New teachers taking over successful music programs should prioritize which of the following behaviors?

a. Establishing their own protocols to demonstrate that there is new leadership
b. Establishing contact with parents to inform them of a change in the program
c. Establishing contact with the outgoing director to ease the transition
d. Establishing a needed budget for capital and operating expenses

42. Which of the following choral structures is the most common for four-part vocal harmony?

a. SATB
b. SAB
c. SSAA
d. TTBB

43. Which of the following reasons best explains why clarinets are tuned slightly sharp by the manufacturer?

a. Manufacturing the clarinet slightly sharp helps players perform all the tones throughout the register more closely to well-tempered tuning.
b. If a clarinet naturally plays flat with all joints pushed in, there is no easy remedy to put the instrument in tune.
c. Because there are options for purchasing shorter barrels based upon the manufacturer's design.
d. Performing slightly sharp is less abrasive on the listener's ear than performing flat.

44. What is one reason why there is a movement in lower elementary general music classes to replace teaching soprano recorder with ukulele?

a. The ukulele is an accompanying instrument
b. The ukulele sounds better in a group setting
c. The ukulele is easier to learn than the recorder
d. The ukulele is more culturally relevant in society

45. Which of the following techniques for achieving blend in an alto saxophone section is the most practical factor in getting the section to perform so that there is one homogenous blend of sound?

a. Have all students play with the same ligature.
b. Have all students play with reeds of similar strength.
c. Have all students play the same brand instrument.
d. Have all students play with similarly constructed mouthpieces.

46. When using rating scales, checklists, and holistic rubrics to measure and evaluate individual achievement within group performance, which of the following techniques is most related to helping students grow musically?

a. Assign each student to self-assess their musical strengths and weaknesses.
b. Use a checklist to ensure appropriate posture and instrument holding.
c. Grade students on attendance and perceived participation.
d. Use peers to assess each student's musical achievement.

47. Taking in a deep breath over as many counts as possible, holding the breath, and then slowly letting out the air on an "S" sound, over as many counts as possible, is an example of what kind of vocal warm-up?

a. Octave warm-up
b. Falsetto warm-up
c. Tessitura warm-up
d. Breathing warm-up

48. Which of the following discipline principles is most related to achieving good classroom management throughout an entire school?

a. Each classroom has a different set of rules depending upon the class and teacher's style.
b. Each teacher has an emergency clause that, when invoked, brings severe consequences.
c. Each teacher uses various disciplinary techniques depending upon the situation.
d. Each classroom has the same core classroom rules.

49. A beginning cello student plays with too much arm movement; what is most likely causing the problem?

a. The student's back is slouched.
b. The elbow is not bending properly on a bow stroke.
c. The thumb is placed too close to the second and third fingers.
d. The fingers are overly curved.

50. The Middle Eastern *maqam* system of melodic organization is most similar to which aspect of Western music theory?

a. Counterpoint
b. Binary form
c. Modes
d. Notation

51. Compared to other leaders in music education, which of the following theories about learning is most related to Orff Schulwerk?

a. Music is a language
b. Ontologic follows phylogenic
c. There must be a systematic method
d. Teaching must be based on Piaget's model of child development

52. When teaching trumpet, which of the following is the best time to teach the third valve slide adjustment for intonation?

a. As soon as possible
b. After two to four years of playing
c. Advanced high school
d. Preparation for college music majors

53. What is the standard instrumentation of the concert band as prescribed by members of the American Bandmasters Association?

a. Two flutes, two oboes, two bassoons, three clarinets, one bass clarinet, four saxophones, four horns, three trumpets, three trombones, one baritone horn, one tuba, and three or four percussion instruments
b. Four violins, four violas, four cellos, four basses, two piccolos, one English horn, one harp, one bass trombone, one bassoon, one contrabassoon, and two saxophones
c. Four flutes, two piccolos, three oboes, one bassoon, two contrabassoons, four clarinets, three alto clarinets, two bass clarinets, one saxophone, and two percussion instruments
d. Two French horns, two flugelhorns, three trumpets, two cornets, one baritone horn, two tubas, three trombones, three saxophones, and four percussion instruments

54. Which of the following music notation labels are represented in the illustration?

a. Two types of tablature clefs
b. Two types of octave clefs
c. Two types of neutral clefs
d. Two types of treble clefs

55. Which of the following rationales best justifies a teacher who advocates for beginning trumpet players to use both letter names and tonal syllables when learning songs by rote, by ear, and by notation?

a. It prevents students from being confused with multiple systems.
b. It makes transposition easier than using note names and steps.
c. It makes the learning of music reading much faster.
d. It makes transfer to other brass instruments easier.

56. How should cymbals be stored?

a. Upright in a sturdy and stiff box
b. Stacked in a dark closet or room
c. Flat in a soundproof and clean locker
d. Divided in padded bags or cases

57. Which of the following elements is NOT audiated by students?

a. Intervals
b. Melodic contour
c. Time signatures
d. Harmonic functions

58. The pyramid model of balance and blend in a vocal ensemble refers to what theory?

a. Louder singers should sing at the same level as softer singers.
b. Higher-pitched singers should sing softer than the lowest pitched singers.
c. Taller singers should stand behind shorter singers.
d. Melodic singers should sing louder than accompanying singers.

59. Which of the following steps for a middle-D not "speaking" correctly on a saxophone should be done first when diagnosing this problem?

a. Look at the G# key to see if it's stuck.
b. Examine the octave key mechanism.
c. Play just the reed/mouthpiece setup.
d. Run a leak light to check for pad seating.

60. If a singer does not control the rate of exhalation, what common problem happens physically when the singer runs out of breath?

a. The diaphragm contracts.
b. The abdominals tighten.
c. The chest collapses.
d. The pharynx dilates.

61. Which of the following is the most fundamental tool for beginning improvisation?

a. Syncopation
b. Imitation
c. Modulation
d. Inversion

62. Which of the following cooperative learning techniques, when used in a chamber orchestra rehearsal setting, best promotes positive musical interdependence among group members?

a. Assign students to critique their own sections' strengths and weaknesses.
b. Have each section perform all of the other sections' parts to the extent possible.
c. Task each student to keep an individual rehearsal diary, documenting how the group improves over time.
d. Teach students interpersonal conflict resolution skills in order to prevent hurting group performance quality.

63. A wind ensemble performs a piece in sonata form. How do they achieve beatless sonority when modulating?

a. Instruments performing the fundamental tones use a tuner to play with equal-tempered tuning, and other instruments compromise with embouchure adjustments and alternate fingerings to play with just intonation throughout the key changes.
b. Performers take into account that the equal-tempered tuning system is a compromise and that certain pitches and harmonies will naturally be slightly out-of-tune through key changes.
c. All instruments play with equal-tempered tuning in order to end the movement or piece on the same reference pitch within the key that the piece began.
d. Adjust the entire ensemble's reference pitches to equal temperament throughout the exposition, development, and recapitulation.

64. Which of the following notation programs allows musicians to notate compositions electronically and then transfer the data to other MIDI instruments?

a. Mozarteum
b. Sibelius
c. MagicNote
d. Forte Score

65. Which of the following is an example of *absolute music*, as opposed to *program music*?

a. *Symphony No. 5* by Ludwig van Beethoven
b. *Don Quixote* by Richard Strauss
c. *Danse Macabre* by Camille Saint-Saëns
d. *Symphonie Fantastique* by Hector Berlioz

66. Which of the following Western music subgenres is this 20th century music excerpt from?

a. Neoclassical
b. Impressionism
c. Minimalism
d. Serialism

67. What is NOT a typical instrument of Appalachian folk music?

a. Dulcimer
b. Banjo
c. Tumbadora
d. Mandolin

68. The following music excerpt was composed by which of the following composers?

a. Carl Orff
b. Igor Stravinsky
c. Aaron Copland
d. Dmitri Shostakovich

69. Which pop musician directly references the excerpt of this Chopin Prelude?

a. Stevie Wonder
b. Ray Charles
c. John Legend
d. Billy Joel

70. Which of the following jazz standards is performed in the bossa nova style?

a. "Desafinado"
b. "What Is This Thing Called Love"
c. "Cherokee"
d. "How High the Moon"

71. Which of the following speech, movement, and pattern sequences best represents an elementary-level Orff rhythm teaching sequence?

a. Speech, movement
b. Unmetered speech, poetry
c. Pantomime, free movement
d. Double moving ostinatos, pitched drone

72. Which of the following music terms is best defined as an ornament or embellishment in which the performed note is first brushed—as in a flam—by the note just above it before playing that note for almost its entire value?

a. Acciaccatura
b. Appoggiatura
c. Upper mordent
d. Tremolo

73. Which of the following conducting patterns best fits the music excerpt?

(Elgar Enigma Variations VII Op. 36)

a. 

b. 

c. 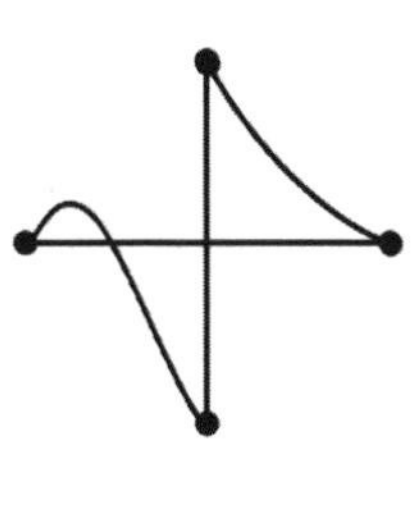

d. 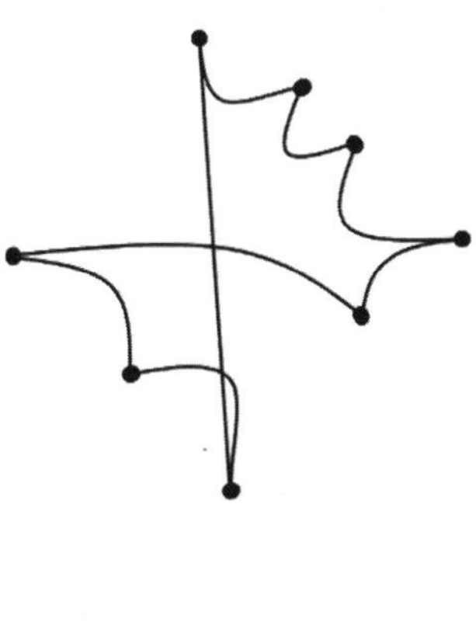

74. What is the top range of flute parts in published band music that is graded level I?

a. A5
b. C6
c. G5
d. D5

75. Which of the following ensemble rehearsal pacing shapes is the most appropriate representation for the usual flow of intensity of an ensemble rehearsal?

a. 

b. 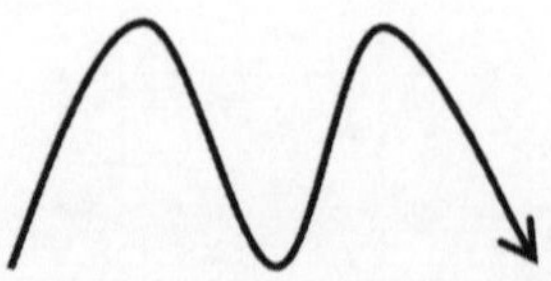

c. 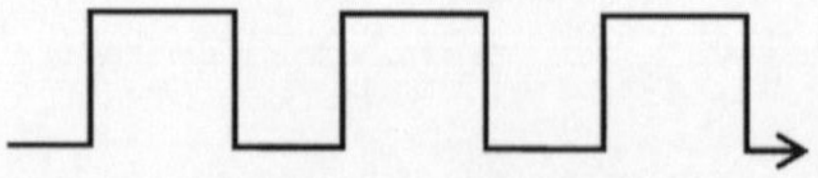

d. 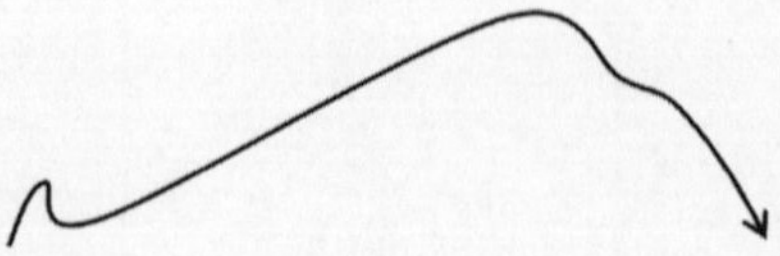

76. When using drones to improve intonation, which of the following sequences is most appropriate for clarinets to use in order to develop technique and audiation skill in their individual practice sessions?

a. Tune to an octave, tune to a perfect fifth.
b. Tune to an octave, tune to a major third.
c. Tune to a perfect fifth, tune to a major third.
d. Tune to a perfect fifth, tune to a 12th overblow.

77. Which of the following techniques for determining the size of a violin or viola is most appropriate to use for beginning players?

a. Measure from the base of the neck to the wrist, arm being diagonal to the floor and at a 45-degree angle.
b. Measure from the base of the neck to the center of the palm, arm being diagonal to the floor and at a 45-degree angle.
c. Stand and hold the instrument upright, positioning it against the left side, holding the neck with the fingers in first position where the fingers line up with the eyes.
d. Choose the right-sized chair so that there is a 90-degree angle in the legs, set the endpin around 12 inches off the ground, and the instrument should rest on the chest at a 45-degree angle with the C string peg being near the left ear.

78. What is one reason why ukuleles might be used in general music classrooms instead of guitars?

a. Guitars are less prone to damage in low humidity
b. Guitars are generally more expensive
c. Guitars are less preferred by students
d. Guitars have a more restricted range of tone

79. Which of the following composers arranged the piece exemplified by the music excerpt for orchestra?

a. Hindemith
b. Stravinsky
c. Orff
d. Ravel

80. Which of the following program evaluation techniques is most useful when done at the state or even national level, rather than the local level?

a. Well-seasoned subject matter experts (SMEs) make judgments about the worth of a program.
b. Standardized tests of music achievement are administered to students in all music classes.
c. Administrators make professional development recommendations based upon contest results.
d. Music advocacy groups write standards and make recommendations for materials and equipment.

Answer Key and Explanations for Test #1

1. C: The publisher is not an aspect of the score the conductor needs to learn when preparing a score; however, the form, transpositions, and dynamics of the score are all necessary aspects of the score to learn when preparing a score for rehearsals and performances.

2. A: Singing root harmonies helps students to lock in singing in-tune, and provides the context of harmonic function for students to use while learning to audiate and sing harmony.

3. D: A loud, forceful, and fast sound tends to convey passion, answer D. Sorrow tends to be represented by slower sounds; calm is usually represented by slower, light sounds; and hope tends to be represented by sustained, high sounds.

4. D: Option D is the correct answer because teachers can group by student preferences when offering choices of tunes or songs that students want to learn, such as learning about the history and use of the guitar in different cultural settings or genres and then having the different groups of students present their findings and perform to the rest of the class. Option A is incorrect because high and low achievers can both learn from one another (often more than they do from the teacher), even when differentiating instruction, such as progressing with tonal and rhythm patterns through Gordon's skill learning sequence, or when assigning students different tunes or songs to learn as homework in order to play for the class. Option B is incorrect because formative assessment assists the teacher in deciding how to differentiate instruction based upon achievement and preferences. Option C is incorrect because it is impractical to provide individual lessons to each student. A better option is to pair high achievers with low achievers for peer coaching.

5. A: Kodály advocated beginning with intervals within the pentatonic scale, as his observational research of children was that, during play, children most often chanted *so-mi*, or *so-mi-la*. This is different from singing—think "Ring Around the Rosie," or "na-na-na-na-na-na," which are chants, not songs. Also, Hungarian folk music often incorporated pentatony (with Hungarian-placed intervals). Kodály also believed that half-steps were difficult for children to sing.

6. C: Options A, B, and D should be a part of that initial checklist. Other preparations should be procuring music and teaching materials, procuring or designating performance attire and rules for behavior, arranging for chaperones, and making plans for the concerts to be recorded, among other plans.

7. C: The Romantic period. Partly as a response to the widely perceived dominance of German music and composers during the Classical period that preceded it, the Romantic period is most strongly associated with musical nationalism; that is, composers from a given nation wrote music meant to invoke their native lands, peoples, and cultures. Noted examples include the music of Bedřich Smetana, Antonín Dvořák, and Jean Sibelius. While the other periods—Baroque, Classical, and Contemporary—would have seen selected composers and pieces which could be argued as nationalistic, the Romantic period *most strongly* is associated with musical nationalism and is therefore the correct answer.

8. B: Beginning clarinet players have not yet mastered the embouchure development or technical skills required to play the lowest notes of the clarinet or to play over the break. G4 allows the performer to establish the basis for the clarinet performing in tune with itself (because the note is an open note between the barrel and the first joint), as well as secure a reference pitch from the ensemble. G4's pitch tendency is sharp. G3 uses the left-hand assembly and allows the player to continue to place the instrument in tune with itself because it does not affect the left-hand portion of the clarinet. Options (A), (C), and (D) are incorrect because either the notes are too low, go over the break, begin with the right hand, or some combination of these.

9. B: The wah-wah mute, also known by the brand name Harmon mute, produces a buzzed tone and is often associated with Miles Davis during his cool jazz period. The straight mute results in a tinny, metallic sound; the cup mute produces a muffled, darker tone; and the bucket mute produces a softer tone and reduces the piercing quality of loud or high notes that can be amplified by other mutes.

10. D: A quaver is equal to an eighth note. Every time a descriptor term is added, it cuts the note value in half (e.g., a semiquaver is equal to a 16th note).

11. D: Brass instruments typically produce sound through the buzzing of the player's lips as the air travels through the instrument. The lips act as a vibrating valve that produces oscillating air and pressure. Changes in dynamics for the brass instruments are a product of the volume of air moving through the instrument. Embouchure primarily impacts tone and pitch. Frequency refers to the frequency of a sound wave, which determines pitch. Posture can impact pitch, tone, or volume, but the volume of air has a more direct impact on dynamics than posture.

12. A: The US Department Office for Civil Rights, within the "Restraint and Resource Document" published by the US Department of Education, describes two types of restraint: physical and mechanical. Option B is incorrect because "physical escort means a temporary touching or holding of the hand, wrist, arm, shoulder, or back for the purpose of inducing a student who is acting out to walk to a safe location" (p.10). Options C describes a form of mechanical restraint, which is a device used to restrict a student's freedom of movement. Option D describes vehicle safety restraints, which are not considered mechanical restraints when used as intended for transport.

13. B: The cha-cha-cha is an onomatopoeia of the musical rhythm: two eighth notes followed by a quarter note. The tresillo is comprised of triplets over a composite duple beat. The son montuno is comprised of a 2-3 clave, and the rumba rhythmic pattern consists of 16th and quarter note beats in triple- and duple-pulses.

14. C: The correlation between general IQ and various musical aptitudes is between 0.10 and 0.20. In other words, one cannot be predicted from the other. Option A is incorrect because it is a popular stereotype that is often perpetuated by teachers who find it difficult to accommodate teaching musical instruments to students with cognitive impairment. Option B is incorrect because there is a low correlation between the potential to achieve in music (audiationally) and general IQ. Option D is incorrect because, for example, there may be a lot of students at the elementary age level who have not yet learned to sing in tune, or may have had limited exposure to music, but may have high potential to achieve in music. That is, in part, why music teachers use music aptitude tests: to help them see what they may not be hearing.

15. D: Mixers allow for more control of the input into a computer. Mixers commonly have volume faders, equalizers, and built-in effects such as reverb and delay, and many have an analog-to-digital converter built in. Mixers are therefore better for recording studio use, but because they are less portable, generally more expensive, and more complicated to use than audio interfaces, they may not be the best choice for use in remote recording.

16. C: When encountering a difficult passage, musicians most effectively practice that passage slowly and thoughtfully. Playing through a challenging passage quickly can be detrimental to the learning process. Studying away from the instrument and practicing the sections before and after can be helpful, but will not address the difficult passage in the most effective manner.

17. B: Dynamic microphones do not need a phantom power source. Although condenser microphones are more sensitive, they generally cannot handle the high sound pressure levels that dynamic microphones are made to handle.

18. B: Edwin Gordon's music learning theory evolved from early leaders in music education, including Suzuki, Dalcroze, and Kodály, but he has also been influenced by White, Gagné, Piaget, and Vygotsky, among others. Gordon's method primarily focused on understanding music as a whole by listening and improving auditory recognition and prediction skills, then honing in on how to perform or read music. Gordon coined the term "audiation," which refers to the internalization of music perception. Audiation plays a central role in Gordon's music learning theory.

19. B: The standard English horn sounds a fifth lower than notated, so it is considered a transposing instrument in F. Other double reed instruments include the oboe and bassoon, both pitched in C and sound as written.

20. C: Pitch is the musical term meaning the frequency of the sound wave of a given musical note. Tempo (A) is the musical term meaning the relative speed of a piece of music, i.e., how slowly or quickly it should be played. Melody (B) is a tune, which is made up of a series of different pitches. Rhythm (D) is both the overall time signature of a musical piece, i.e., how many beats each measure contains, and also the patterns created by varying and repeating the durations of individual notes.

21. D: A synchronization (or "synch") license allows the licensee to synchronize music to visual images or recordings. A grand license is obtained for the production of large dramatic works, such as the yearly performance of a school musical. A mechanical license is obtained when someone wishes to cover a song that someone else holds copyright to. A compulsory license allows someone to cover a previously released recording of someone else's song that is copyrighted, provided royalties are paid.

22. C: The overtone series can be best understood within the context of physics, the study of matter and its motion through space and time. The concept of overtones refers to a specific acoustic property of sound. For every one frequency, there are multiple other frequencies, or overtones, that vibrate through the resonant space of its normal modes.

23. B: Nationalism, as the name implies, was the name of the movement in the Romantic era in which composers used folk melodies of their country within their compositions. Impressionism focused on capturing the moods and emotions of a subject though texture, musical "color," ambiguous harmony, among other techniques. Romanticism focused on music that portrayed fantastical, emotional, and dramatic subjects. Realism was primarily an artistic and literary movement that focused on portraying subjects in a non-idealized, realistic style.

24. D: The idea that students learn by playing games and working with content and skills without explicitly being told that they are learning a particular tune or song is valuable because it makes learning fun and helps the student to learn more quickly. For example, when teaching students to learn a song at the elementary level, asking them to do four or five things, such as identify repeated rhythm patterns or words, or describe the meaning of the song, helps the student to learn the song in just a few repetitions.

Option A is incorrect because a gestalt is defined—there is no exact translation in English—as the sum being greater, or different, than the parts. Some of these techniques, such as asking students to identify the tonality or meter of a song that is being sung to them for the first time, do help to create a gestalt. But, some activities, such as remembering the first word of a song, simply help to teach the song without students being aware that they are learning it. Option B is incorrect because, while teacher modeling does help students learn the song while absorbing musical behavior, it is not the primary purpose of using this teaching technique. Option C is incorrect because, while the activity is efficient and enjoyable, the students are not always learning by rote. Rote learning is defined as learning without full understanding (e.g., students might not know the meter or tonality of the tune/song). It is usually achieved by memorization through repetition.

25. D: The twelfth bar. In the twelve-bar blues form (also jazz) the turnaround refers to the passage at the end of one section that leads to the next section. Twelve-bar compositions are typically arranged with the first four measures under the I chord. The next four measures are split typically between the IV chord and the I chord. The final set of four bars leads to some combination of the I, IV, and V chords, which compels the listener to "turnaround" to another set of twelve bars. Given that the turnaround would come at the end of the collection of measures, answers A through C would, by definition, be incorrect.

26. A: This Requiem excerpt was composed by Wolfgang Mozart. Mozart was almost certainly influenced by Michael Haydn's *Requiem*. In turn, Hector Berlioz's *Dies Irae* is said to rival the magnificence of Mozart's *Requiem*. Robert Schumann proclaimed Cherubini's (a contemporary of Mozart) *Requiem* as being "without equal," and Beethoven requested that Cherubini's be played at his own funeral.

27. B: The gamelan ensemble is the traditional ensemble music of Javanese, Sundanese, and Balinese in Indonesia. The gamelan orchestra contains tuned percussion instruments like bells, gongs, drums, and metallophones. It is used for celebratory, religious, and political purposes.

28. D: Girls' singing voices change just as boys' do. While the change may begin earlier—as is the case with most of a girl's adolescent development—and is subtler, it does indeed take place. Girls who wish to sing through early adolescence and beyond will need the coaching of a good, patient instructor. Because girls' voices change, (A) and (B) are incorrect. Also incorrect is (C). Boys, like girls, can make good music in elementary and middle school, regardless of the changes taking place in their voices.

29. B: This excerpt is the first movement of Franz Joseph Haydn's Symphony No. 24. This music is balanced, relatively diatonic, not overly ornamental, lacking in overt emotional expression, and without much polyphony. The instrumentation, stylization, and harmonic content are not indicative of the Romantic or Neoclassical periods.

30. C: The chin is flat, and even concave, much like it might be when applying lipstick or spitting an apple seed that is caught in the teeth. The corners of the lips are firm, pulled back, and may be pointed slightly downward. Once these two factors are accounted for, the embouchure should naturally fall into place. The next steps are learning how to buzz, then where to place the mouthpiece on the lips and the positioning of the tongue (if it does not come naturally to the player). This basic embouchure technique is also applicable to woodwind instruments, although woodwind instrument embouchures add steps in determining the shape of the lips ("oh")— just like a string at the top opening of a bag is pulled from both sides—and adjusting the lips when placing the mouthpiece or reed inside the mouth. The woodwind embouchure adds steps to the basic formation because, unlike the brass embouchure in which the lips are the sound maker, a reed or double reed is needed to make the sound with woodwinds.

31. B: Backwards design was created to improve learning outcomes by explicitly creating those outcomes first, rather than simply creating activities and then the assessment, which leads to poor achievement of goals and objectives. Evidence-centered design (ECD) is about ensuring that the evidence of achievement is planned before creating learning activities and experiences that lead students to the achievement of those goals and objectives.

32. D: A conductor's elbow should be positioned so that it is slightly raised away from the body. The baton can then be best and clearly seen from all angles. It should not be raised high above the podium, close to the torso, nor pointed to the front of the ensemble; the baton should be a natural extension of the hand and arm.

33. A: Students who can solfege have an easier time transposing between clefs than students who must transpose by counting up or down a whole step. Additionally, learning to read and perform from both clefs using solfege reinforces solfege skill. Option B is incorrect because that option reinforces the idea that beginning students should learn only treble clef. Option C is incorrect because it is based on the assumption that if the trumpet reads only treble clef, then the beginning baritone player should read only treble clef. Instead, the teacher should consider the comprehensive development of musicianship and the idea that learning to transpose becomes more difficult over time, rather than easier as a student gets older. Option D is incorrect because using treble clef increases the use of ledger lines as a student becomes more experienced.

Learning science informs us that:

1. Initially, learning is a process of using the concepts of same and different. Performing in two clefs produces notes that look different but sound the same.
2. When beginning students learn both clefs simultaneously and comparatively using solfege, the true confusion of transposition that occurs after a student has become used to reading only one clef is alleviated. Analogously, the student can read in two dimensions instead of one.
3. Students should be learning how to use tonal syllables (solfege) to promote audiation in general music class, particularly when taught by Orff, Kodály, and Gordon teachers. Thus, *do-re-mi*, etc. in major tonality sounds the same no matter what key it is in and how it is notated because the syntax is the same; if students know through audiation that *do-re-mi* (for example) sounds the same but looks different in various keys, they should be taught to read with solfege in various keys and tonalities (e.g., moveable *do*, *la*-based minor, or *so*-based Mixolydian).

34. D: When harmonizing any given melody, analysis should first be done before any planning, sketching, or execution of harmonization. The musician should first observe the contour of the melody and analyze what possible harmonies can be written with regard to the pitches and rhythmic structure.

35. D: While individual players' characteristic sounds are unique due to factors ranging from oral cavity to the mouthpiece and instrument being played, there is a general consensus by musicians, musical instrument manufacturers, and music teachers about what a particular instrument's characteristic sound should be. This is evinced by the relatively homogenous sound that most quality instruments produce by players with good embouchures, appropriate breath support, and quality articulation. Intonation is the next factor in the sequence because a section or ensemble cannot achieve blend or balance unless players are performing with instruments that are in tune with themselves and when the players are playing in tune with other members of the ensemble. Blend is related to a characteristic sound and the combination of characteristic sounds within, between, and among sections in order to create a homogenous and sonorous (if not unique) group sound that is different than any individual's characteristic sound. The next factor in the sequence, balance, is primarily a matter of each instrumentalist performing at appropriate volume levels in relation to the sound that they contribute to the section and ensemble.

36. A: Depressing the trigger opens up additional tubing. The principle is that the bigger the instrument, the lower the sound. When using the trigger, the lowest fundamental pitch on the instrument goes from Bb to F.

37. C: Option C is correct because the continuous motion of this excerpt demonstrates the stylistic characteristic of being composed during the Baroque era. Options A and B are incorrect; while basso continuo and polyphonic textures are defining characteristics of the Baroque era, they are not illustrated in this excerpt. Option D is incorrect because this characteristic is more related to music composed in the Classical era.

38. C: Part of the tonal audiation and writing subtest requires students to listen to harmonic progressions under (or over) a melody and, using chord function symbols, write the harmonic functions that they are hearing. Option D is incorrect because students are not required to improvise within the ITML.

39. D: Option D is the correct answer because teachers do not want a floor or ceiling effect when working to teach to individual strengths and weakness. An arbitrary point that demonstrates minimal competency can be established at any point along the rating scale, and grades can also be arbitrarily derived along the continuum of the rating scale.

If, for example, a student scored a 6 on this ratings scale, there would be no room for that student to grow, and the teacher could not identify individual strengths and weaknesses in order to help the student improve his musicianship. Option B is incorrect because, while this is a single-dimensional rating scale, that alone does not help to teach to individual differences.

Performances that require the use of multiple rating scales (e.g., tonal, rhythmic, and expressive) can employ multiple judges in order to avoid the halo effect and so that each rating scale can be properly attended to. Or, one judge can record the performance anonymously (to avoid bias) and rate the performance for each rating scale 5-10 days apart. This takes time, but measurement and evaluation of student achievement have become high stakes. Thus, properly measuring performances is integral to the teaching and learning process and is the primary component of the teaching and learning process in evidence-centered design.

40. A: Weight and flow are most directly changed in this example. Laban's model related elements of bodily movement to creativity and described four continuums to taxonomize elements of motion. This was used to inspire creativity in students by having them experience paradoxical scenarios, such as "picking up a teacup filled with liquid lead." This causes the students to respond imaginatively to an unrealistic scenario. The continuums related to each of Laban's effort elements are:

FLOW
Bound - - - - - - - - - - Free
SPACE
Direct - - - - - - - - - - Indirect
WEIGHT
Heavy - - - - - - - - - - Light
TIME
Slow - - - - - - - - - - Fast

When changing the liquid in a pretend teacup from water to lead, the weight becomes heavier. This weight change makes the flow of the cup become more bound. The timing and the space are unaffected.

41. C: Procuring information about an established program helps to ensure a smooth transition. Topics to be discussed include fundraising, student make-up, student leadership positions, previous concert programs and repertoire, organization handbook, and the booster organization, among other topics.

42. A: The most common choral structure for four-part vocal harmony is SATB (soprano, alto, tenor, bass). SAB only makes use of three voices, and SSAA and TTBB are not as commonly used as SATB.

43. B: There is one remedy for a clarinet that plays flat, and it is costly: purchasing a shorter barrel. Therefore, clarinets are typically tuned slightly sharp by the manufacturer.

44. A: Option A is correct because students can learn to accompany themselves while singing songs. Option B is incorrect because both the recorder and the ukulele can sound pleasant in group settings. (In particular, see Richard Grunow and Edwin Gordon's *Jump Right in: The Instrumental Series* for recorder. It teaches the recorder while also teaching audiation, which improves recorder performance.) Option C is incorrect because this is a subjective rationale: there has been little or no published objective experimental research that justifies this statement. Option D is incorrect because both the ukulele and the soprano recorder can be used in an Orff Instrumentarium. The recorder has a long history in Western European music, beginning in the Middle Ages, and continues to be popular throughout the country and in American culture.

45. D: While a combination of all of the options in relationship to the individual player contributes to the type of sound being made, the configuration of the mouthpiece tip, lay, rails, and particularly the baffle contribute more to the sound than the other options, and at a more practical and cheaper price, especially when asking all students to play on the same brand and model instrument, which is not very practical.

A baffle can be a "flat" baffle (producing a darker, thicker, warmer sound with less projection); a "roll-over" baffle (producing a middle-of-the-road sound); or a "step" baffle (producing brighter, louder, and a more projected sound). A flat baffle allows more air to pass through the mouthpiece at once, but at a slower speed. A step baffle is curved, which speeds up the airflow but allows less air to travel through the mouthpiece at once.

46. A: Students are most interested in improving their own musicianship and, when given the opportunity, will use rating scales, rubrics, and checklists that are based upon technical and musical factors to self-evaluate their own achievement. Further, there are technical and musical factors listed on standardized adjudication sheets for band, orchestra, choir, show choir, and others that students can use to improve their personal musicianship as well as their musicianship within an ensemble. All students should have copies of these adjudication sheets, as they have the right to know what they will be measured on and how they will be evaluated. The music teacher's responsibility is to help students explore and learn about tuning, intonation, balance, blend, bowing, pronunciation, and enunciation (all the factors on these adjudication sheets) in order to empower students to assess their own strengths and weaknesses. Thus, a music teacher must be musical; a technician on all instruments (including the voice); and be able to communicate, model, diagnose, and prescribe based on the factors on the adjudication sheets, both in individual and group settings. Measuring, evaluating, and grading students based upon attendance and perceived participation is relatively easy in a group setting but does little to promote musical growth. While ensuring appropriate posture and instrument holding is important, allowing students to self-assess their strengths and weaknesses more directly affects musical growth. Using peers who often are lacking in knowledge and skills to assess others could lead to resentment or a lack of group cohesion.

47. D: This is an example of a breathing warm-up. Breathing warm-ups engage the diaphragm for supported singing and help to warm the vocal cords for singing.

48. D: At the heart of a discipline (teaching) program should be a small number of core rules that every classroom shares. This ensures that students know what to expect consistently throughout the day. While there may also be an "emergency clause" that can be invoked in exigent circumstances, that is not the glue that provides the needed cohesive structure for student expectations throughout the school.

49. B: A beginning cello student who plays with too much arm movement is most likely not bending the elbow properly on a bow stroke. When bowing on a cello, students should use not only their upper arms, but also their forearms, elbows, wrists, hands, and fingers as well. A stiff elbow causes too much arm movement during a bow stroke.

50. C: The *maqam* system of melodic organization used in Middle Eastern music most resembles the Western mode. There are more than 30 different *maqamat*, and each defines the melodic contour, pitches, and hierarchical development of the scale.

51. B: Orff seemed to have a general belief that individual human development (ontology) followed the development of the species (phylogeny). That is, at least in part, why he called simple songs "elemental music." This is also why a strong and pronounced rhythmic drive that impels motion and emotion plays a dominant role in his music and thinking about how to engage children in music. One can hear this in his compositions (e.g., *Carmina Burana*). Orff's primary thinking about elemental music is related to the idea that music and movement are elemental modes of expression first and foremost, and that creating an approach to music exploration, performance, and learning based upon this helps children to discover themselves and who they are in relation to people and nature around them. Piaget, among others, was influenced by the 18th century idea of development described in option b), and his stage theory of childhood development reflects this. Option c) is incorrect because Orff did not create a systematic method (what a teacher does, why she does it, and when) so much as an approach for children to discover and create music in order to enrich themselves throughout their lives.

52. A: Even when teaching with traditional, non-audiation-based method books and learning first to decode notes on a staff with letter names, students should learn to pull out their third valve slide. In the same way that many teachers use tape on the fretboard to help string players play in tune even when they cannot audiate, trumpet teachers should be engaging in kinesthetic training as well as establishing good performance habits. If a teacher implements audiation-based methods and techniques into beginning instrumental music lessons, the student will generally not tolerate performing out of tune.

53. A: The American Bandmasters Association prescribed the concert band as having parts for two flutes, two oboes, two bassoons, three clarinets, one bass clarinet, four saxophones, four horns, three trumpets, three trombones, one baritone horn, one tuba, and three or four percussion instruments. The brass, woodwind family, and percussion instrument families are all represented.

54. C: A neutral clef is used for non-pitched instruments. When notating percussion, each line represents a specific instrument. If there is only one non-pitched instrument, a single staff line may be used.

55. B: Teaching students to audiate with tonal syllables (moveable *do*, *la*-based minor) and to use those tonal syllables (if needed) when singing a part or when transposing on their instrument allows them to perform tunes and songs learned by rote, by ear, and by notation in any key. Additionally, when students become more advanced in high school, they may use melodies, such as the primary melody in Bach's "Jesu, Joy of Man's Desiring" as a flow and expressive exercise.

56. D: Cymbals should be stored divided in padded bags or cases, if possible. They should never be stacked directly on top of each other, or upright on their edges, for the risk of damage. The padding helps to protect the cymbal metal and to prolong the life of each cymbal.

57. C: Students audiate musical meter and tonality—they internally hear and feel patterns of beat, tonal center, scale degrees, intervals in context, melodic contour, and harmonic functions (e.g., tonic vs. dominant). Time signatures, however, are notation symbols that label meter on the page; they are not perceived directly in inner hearing. Thus, time signatures are not audiated, while the other options are.

58. B: The pyramid model of balance and blend refers to the theory that higher pitched singers and instruments should play softer than the lowest pitched singers and instruments so that an ideal balance exists between the treble and the bass. In this model, the higher pitched section will also be able to hear the bass for better intonation and blend.

59. C: For almost all saxophone-related problems, playing just the reed/mouthpiece setup is the first step in diagnosing a problem. In the case of a middle-D not speaking, if the reed/mouthpiece setup is working, the problem is usually that the octave key mechanism is not working and may need to be bent back into position.

60. C: If a singer does not control the rate of exhalation, a collapsed chest is a common problem that happens. After the inhalation, the singer must control the rate of exhalation, as the flow of air through the vocal cords results in sound. The singer must use great care to manage the rate of airflow by engaging the abdominal muscles to achieve a steady stream of air through the trachea and larynx.

61. B: Imitation is a foundational tool for beginning improvisation. Imitation allows students to learn techniques, progressions, melodic contour, and rhythmic patterns of improvisers of the past.

Once students have immersed themselves in studying imitation, they will be much better suited to assimilate improvisation techniques for new musical ideas.

62. B: Option B is correct; when each section learns the other sections' parts, they are made more sensitive to listening and adjusting their performance based upon what they hear when playing together. Options A and C are not cooperative learning techniques that lead to positive interdependence. Option D is a cooperative learning technique, but it is geared more toward social interaction rather than musical interdependence.

63. A: Because sonata form modulates to different keys (and tonalities), if the ensemble is to perform using beatless just intonation, it is impossible for all instrumentalists to perform to their own instrument's compromised tuning system, which resembles as close as possible the compromise of equal temperament made among the 12 tones that instrument manufacturers make. Also, because sonata form ends in the original key, it is important for ensembles to avoid straying too far from equal temperament in order to end a piece with the same fundamental reference pitches in the original key. Thus, it is important for instrumentalists who play the fundamental tones within a key (e.g., the tonic) to stay as close to equal temperament as possible throughout key and tonality changes, while other players compromise and adjust to the changes throughout. In the end, it must be acknowledged that tuning is a matter of compromise in order to perform beatless harmonies.

64. B: Sibelius is notation software that allows musicians to notate compositions electronically and then transfer the data to other MIDI instruments. Other similar programs include MuseScore, Dorico, and Finale. Using notation software helps to reinforce musical concepts and compositional lessons for students.

65. A: Absolute music is defined as instrumental music that exists apart from extra-musical references. Programmatic music is music that can be represented by non-musical images or ideas. Of the answer choices, only answer A, *Symphony No. 5* by Ludwig van Beethoven, exists apart from extra-musical references.

66. D: Serialism is a subgenre within classical music, specifically the era of 20th century Classical music. This piece, titled *Die Maschine*, Op. 1, was composed by Fritz Heinrich Klein (1892–1977). It was published in 1921, and the style is indicative of serialistic composers' presentation of the twelve tones, which includes the techniques of retrograde, inversion, and transposition.

Twelve-tone music is performed by orchestras using equal temperament, as each note is considered equal in value, with the distance between notes being a significant factor. All 12 pitches are arranged in a specific sequence.

67. C: Typical instruments used in Appalachian music include the banjo, mandolin, guitar, autoharp, American fiddle, fretted dulcimer, dobros, and dulcimer. The tumbadora, another name for the conga, is a drum from Cuba used in mambo, rumba, and many other Latin musical styles.

68. B: Igor Stravinsky premiered his *Le Sacre du printemps* ("*The Rite of Spring*") as a ballet and orchestral concert work on May 29th, 1913. Legend grew that the work stirred up passions to a fever pitch, causing a near riot, although this is not corroborated by contemporary reviews of the piece at the time of performance. One can identify this as *The Rite of Spring* by the above excerpt because of the driving rhythmic force of his fourths chord (Eb7 against E major), the instructions for forceful bowing, and the perceptual arhythmic nature of the excerpt through the use of accents.

69. D: Billy Joel directly quotes from Chopin's Op. 28, No. 15 in Db major ("Raindrop") in his introduction to the song "Souvenir" on the ninth track of his album titled *Streetlife Serenade.*

70. A: "Desafinado," composed by Antonio Carlos Jobim, with lyrics created by Newton Mendonça, is a song in the bossa nova style, and the title means "out of tune" or "off key." The bossa nova style originated in Brazil in the early 1950s and is a subgenre of samba (a Latin dance subgenre), much like bebop is a subgenre of jazz music.

It's helpful to understand the bossa nova style in relation to its origins in samba. The samba is a subgenre of Latin music that is as much social as it is about musical factors. Samba lyrics speak about collective life, particular notable events, persons, and culture. Samba first appeared in Bahia, Brazil, and was known as the music of slaves.

Musically, the samba is usually played with guitar, bass, and drums. It can include other instruments, including orchestral instruments. The samba is livelier than the bossa nova, but is harmonically simpler, with fewer chord extensions and less complex voicings. Bossa nova uses major and minor seventh and 13th chords and is usually softer and smoother in style and sound. It's generally not danced to as the samba is because it has no formal dance steps. Bossa nova is usually slower in tempo than the samba.

Bossa nova is highbrow samba. Its lyrics are more about the individual and the topic is often about love, loneliness, or living a pleasurable life. The singing voice is less formal and opera-like than samba.

71. B: Unmetered speech precedes metered speech. Option A is incorrect because both speech and movement—broad conceptual concepts within a sequence—should be taught simultaneously. Option C is incorrect because unstructured movement precedes themed or structured movement. Option D is incorrect because performing double-moving ostinatos is more difficult than performing simple pitched drones.

72. A: Acciaccatura is an ornament or embellishment that was especially common in the Baroque period, though modern solos and ensemble literature still make use of it. The acciaccatura looks like the following:

73. B: Elgar (1857-1934) was an English composer who wrote *Enigma Variations* in 1899. The above excerpt is from variation seven and the tempo is *presto.* Because of the phrasing characteristics, one may be tempted to conduct the piece in 4/4 like Option C, however, the tempo of the music moves so that the appropriate pattern is a two-beat pattern. The music is not quite fast enough to warrant a one-beat pattern.

74. B: In published band music that is graded level I, C6 is the top range of flute parts. Some beginning flute players, particularly audiators, can use their right-hand pinky finger to perform down to a low C4 and even up to a high G6. Students who use multiple methods, one being a method that teaches audiation (e.g., *Jump Right In: The Instrumental Series*) and the other being a standard lesson book, actually tend to move more quickly through the lesson book, particularly if they are students who have at least average music aptitude. Students with low music aptitude move more slowly through the audiation-based method book and, hence, also through the standard lesson book. To be clear, achievement in audiation and in playing songs by rote and by ear in multiple keys and tonalities drive the executive (technical) skills required to move through standard lesson books. State and local performance standards reflect or are a reflection of published instrument and vocal ranges for every instrument and voice type. In establishing minimum standards, a maximum standard for most students is also established, thus protecting players from bad performance habits or physical harm by extending a range beyond what is physically reasonable.

75. D: The pattern in answer choice D allows for a meaningful introduction and a fast-paced rehearsal that builds to a final climax, creating a gestalt and synergy in group performance at the end of the rehearsal. A "gestalt" may be defined as the whole being greater, or different, than the sum of the parts. A "synergy" is a gestalt that happens when two or more persons work together to create an idea, product, or process.

Option A is incorrect because students need time to become situated to their surroundings and to warm up their voices and instruments. Option B is incorrect because the curve in the middle goes all the way down, de-energizing the class environment (if it didn't go all the way down, it might be a good model to follow, depending on the class circumstances). Option C is just a variant of Option B.

Any class, whether it is physical education, biology, or music, is best when it builds in intensity towards its intended purpose and climax, then allows students time to synthesize and generalize what they have learned. This is often preceded by a summary section toward the end of a lesson.

The short curve up in the beginning of a lesson is the stakeholder exercise, which often provides a hook for students to cognitively and emotionally hook to.

76. A: Octaves, and then perfect fifths, are among the first tones within an instrument's overtone series for students to learn. Option D is incorrect because, although the clarinet overblows at the 12th, the overblow is one of the more complex tones in the instrument's overtone series. All instrumentalists should practice drones starting with the octave and the perfect fifth.

77. B: To determine the appropriate size of a violin or viola, one should measure from the base of the neck to the center of the palm, with the arm diagonal to the floor and at a 45-degree angle. Option A is incorrect because measuring to the wrist is a popular mistake that inexperienced string teachers often make. Option C is the technique for determining the size of a double bass. Option D is for determining the size of the cello. For determining the size of the cello and bass, the size of the hand and length of the arm is also a consideration.

78. B: Option B is correct because quality beginner guitars are significantly more expensive than quality beginner ukuleles. Option A is incorrect because both guitars and ukuleles are made from wood and are subject to cracking in low humidity environments, such as classrooms that are heated throughout the winter months or constantly cooled because of the geographic location. Relatively cheap dehumidifiers may be purchased to keep with these instruments. It should also be noted that keeping these instruments in high humidity can also cause damage. Option C is incorrect because there is no objective evidence or research to validate this statement. Option D is incorrect because guitars have a greater range of tone than ukuleles, which may prompt some music teachers to teach guitar instead of ukulele.

79. D: Modest Mussorgsky's *Pictures at an Exhibition* (1874, a suite of ten pieces plus a variation on the Promenade) was arranged for orchestra by Maurice Ravel in 1922. It was also orchestrated by other composers, such as Sir Henry J. Wood (1915), Leopold Stokowski (1939), and Vladimir Ashkenazy (1982).

80. B: Option B is the correct answer because standardized tests mean that all students are measured using the same material that is delivered in the same way. This provides stakeholders with reasonable access to objective data that indicates how programs, schools, and students are performing. It also is a form of mandate that steers the direction of teaching. The Iowa Tests of Musical Literacy could be used at the national or state levels for program evaluation, rather than at just the local level. Options A and C are incorrect because these are local techniques used in program evaluation. Option D is incorrect because music advocacy groups have relatively little influence at state and national levels.

Practice Test #2

1. Given the following music excerpt, which of the following saxophone fingerings for Bb is most appropriate for fingering the Bb in the first measure?

a. 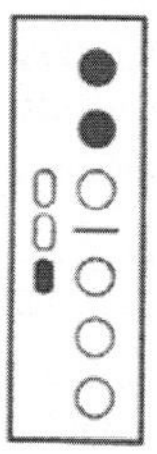

b. 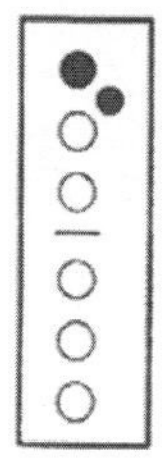

c. 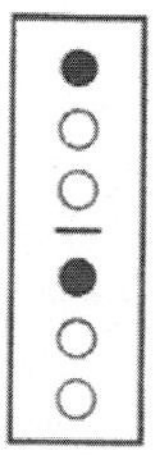

d. 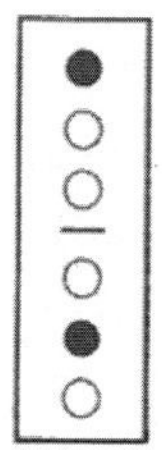

2. When teaching and comparing style and form in an ensemble setting, which of the following explanations is most correct?

a. Forms are subsumed under various styles.
b. Both style and form are largely synonymous.
c. There is a diversity of styles within a particular form.
d. Style represents a time period and form represents musical structure.

3. Which of the following is the most likely cause of a buzzing sound when a beginner snare drum student plays fast?

a. The student is hammering the drumstick onto the drum.
b. The student is playing multiple strokes on the drum.
c. The student is dropping the drumstick onto the drum.
d. The student is playing single strokes on the drum.

4. The Classical era and the Baroque era have distinct stylistic characteristics. Which of the following characteristics displayed in the following excerpt distinguishes it as a Baroque work?

(Bach's Brandenburg Concerto No. 1 in D Major, BWV 1046)

a. Figured bass
b. Changing mood
c. Balanced phrasing
d. Terraced dynamics

5. Which of the following special needs strategies most directly helps special education students who might become easily overwhelmed in the music classroom?

a. Making sure pathways are clear and the room is very organized
b. Providing large-print music books, parts, or scores when possible
c. Modifying instruments, strikers, and bows with tape, sticky dots, and Velcro
d. Incorporating finger warm-ups and breathing exercises into instrumental lessons

6. What physiological changes are happening to pubescent students when their voice "cracks"?

a. The pharynx expands and the uvula hardens.
b. The alveolar ridge thickens and the oral cavity widens.
c. The larynx enlarges and the vocal folds lengthen and thicken.
d. The glottis strengthens and hard palate lowers.

7. As a general rule, how often should a piano be tuned?

a. Once a year
b. Six times a year
c. Every other year
d. Two to four times a year

8. The music excerpt below is an example of which of the following subgenres of early 20th century classical music?

a. Serialist
b. Minimalist
c. Romantic
d. Neoclassical

9. Which of the clefs, tonalities, and keys is the following illustrated melody written in?

a. Bass clef – major – Eb
b. Treble clef – minor – Eb
c. Alto clef – major – Ab
d. Tenor clef – minor – C

10. How do sopranos maximize vocal tract resonance at high frequencies to achieve a vibrant sound?

a. By creating less space in the oral cavity and tightening the vocal tract
b. By creating more space in the oral cavity and relaxing the vocal tract
c. By creating less space in the oral cavity and relaxing the vocal tract
d. By creating more space in the oral cavity and tightening the vocal tract

11. Which of the following improvisational tools is based on a dialogue structure?

a. Repetition
b. Question and answer
c. Syncopation
d. Heterophony

12. How does the hand move when conducting a 4/4 beat pattern?

a. Upward on the first beat, downward on the second beat, inward on the third beat, and outward on the fourth beat
b. Inward on the first beat, outward on the second beat, upward on the third beat, and downward on the fourth beat
c. Outward on the first beat, upward on the second beat, downward on the third beat, and inward on the fourth beat
d. Downward on the first beat, inward on the second beat, outward on the third beat, and upward on the fourth beat

13. The twelve-tone technique of music was created by:

a. Anton Webern
b. Milton Babbit
c. Arnold Schoenberg
d. Pierre Boulez

14. Ostinatos are found extensively in the music of which of the following countries?

a. China
b. Germany
c. Mexico
d. Ethiopia

15. Which three Western music eras can best be described as the time when polyphonic music was developed and reached its peak use?

a. Medieval, Renaissance, Baroque
b. Baroque, Classical, Romantic
c. Classical, Romantic, Impressionist
d. Impressionist, Modern, Post-modern

16. From which of the following countries does the mbira (finger piano) originate?

a. Zimbabwe
b. Japan
c. Peru
d. Chile

17. The rhythms of music are most related to:

a. The size of the canvas in a painting
b. The shape of a sculpture
c. The climax of the plot in a novel
d. The steps taken in dance

18. When overblowing a musical instrument, which of the following overblows at the 12th rather than at the octave?

a. Saxophone
b. Clarinet
c. Trumpet
d. Flute

19. Which of the following two tonalities is this melody best characterized by?

a. Major and Dorian
b. Mixolydian and Aeolian
c. Major and harmonic minor
d. Lydian and melodic minor

20. Which of the following instrument groups would an orchestrator most likely choose to represent a lush canvas of passionate sound?

a. Percussion
b. Strings
c. Brass
d. Woodwinds

21. Which of the following practice techniques is most important for beginning instrumentalists when they practice on their own at home?

a. Many short sessions
b. Breaking music apart
c. Establishing a routine
d. Self-regulated learning

22. Of the following choral settings, which is better suited for homophonic pieces but can make it difficult for the singers to hear other parts?

a. Blocked formation
b. Matrix formation
c. Columnar formation
d. Mixed formation

23. Which of the following ensemble rehearsal descriptions is most important to maximize learning?

a. Alternating between breaking the music down and building it back up
b. Making sure that there is a high play-to-talk ratio
c. Including sight-reading every practice session
d. Slowing rehearsal pace to stay focused

24. Composers typically use which of the following musical modes to convey sadness?

a. Major mode
b. Mixolydian mode
c. Minor mode
d. Lydian mode

25. What is a benefit of having sectional rehearsals as opposed to having only full rehearsals?

a. The players have to clean, adjust, and tune their instruments together.
b. The players are able to work out their counterpoint on original compositions.
c. The players have the opportunity to work on their sight-reading skills.
d. The players are able to fine-tune their parts together.

26. The hymn illustrated below, *Ut queant laxis*, is significant for which of the following reasons?

Translation:

So that your servants may, with loosened voices, resound the wonders of your deeds, clean the guilt from our stained lips, O Saint John.

a. It was used to teach solmization.
b. It was composed for John the Baptist.
c. The melody was composed by Guido d'Arezzo.
d. It was the first example of modern music notation.

27. Which of the following pairs of composers lived and worked during the same time period?

a. Antonio Vivaldi and Frédéric Chopin
b. Gustav Holst and Johann Sebastian Bach
c. Johann Pachelbel and Franz Liszt
d. Pyotr Ilyich Tchaikovsky and Edvard Grieg

28. Which American musical is considered by historians to be the first Broadway musical with a fully integrated, serious, continuous plot?

a. *Cats* by Andrew Lloyd Webber
b. *Show Boat* by Kern and Hammerstein
c. *Ain't Misbehavin'* by Horwitz and Maltby, Jr.
d. *Porgy and Bess* by George Gershwin

29. Competitions for chair positions in a student band or orchestra:

a. should be held daily
b. have no place in the rehearsal space of a music educator in charge of developing musicians' self-esteem
c. should be held at the beginning and end of the semester only
d. should be held both unannounced and on a scheduled basis, at the instructor's discretion

30. Vocal resonance is important for an effective vocal solo performance because:

a. It increases breathing capacity.
b. It simulates harmonic overtones.
c. It creates a well-projected sound.
d. It clarifies vocal diction.

31. Which of the following reasons for using an F attachment on a Bb trombone relates to improving agility?

a. Allows sixth position notes to be played in first position
b. Allows fifth position notes to be played in first position
c. Allows fourth position notes to be played in first position
d. Allows third position notes to be played in first position

32. Mainstreaming and inclusion are concepts included in which of the following parts of the Individuals with Disabilities Education Act (IDEA)?

a. Least restrictive environment (LRE)
b. Free Appropriate Public Education (FAPE)
c. Individualized education program (IEP)
d. Present levels of performance (PLP)

33. Which of the following multicultural music experiences would best lead to an authentic polycultural curriculum?

a. Students are immersed into a way of being by listening, singing, and moving to music in non-Western ways, including styles, tonalities, and meters.
b. Students research heritages of non-Western cultures, then choose to listen to songs and watch ethnological presentations about and prepare food of one of those cultures.
c. Students create a musical drama about the challenges that non-Western peoples might encounter when emigrating to the United States, then do an educational performance for the school population.
d. Students invite a non-Western music performing group to come in and sing, play, and dance for the school population and answer questions that students have as a result of their research about the culture of the invited group.

34. How often should a conductor check for accurate intonation of the ensemble?

a. Only at the beginning of rehearsals
b. Every third rehearsal
c. Periodically during rehearsals
d. At the end of every rehearsal

35. Which of the following vocal ranges represents Gordon's initial audiation range for young children?

a. D5 to A5
b. C4 to G5
c. D4 to A4
d. A4 to F5

36. When an alto saxophone player begins to double on a Bb soprano clarinet, which of the following embouchure differences should be accounted for?

a. The lips should be pulled further back for the clarinet.
b. The mouthpiece should be taken in more for the clarinet.
c. The corners of the embouchure should be firmer for the clarinet.
d. The chin should be more pulled down and concave for the clarinet.

37. Which of the following reasons for administering a standardized timbre preference test is most appropriate for beginning music instrumentalists?

a. To increase student achievement and retention
b. To help balance the instrumentation within a performance ensemble
c. To help students see beyond physical and social attributes that may influence their choice of instrument
d. To help teachers offer harder-to-learn music instruments to students with higher music aptitudes

38. When a student memorizes common practice period rules, such as the four uses of the second inversion tonic chord, which of the following parts of Bloom's taxonomy is being most engaged?

a. Knowledge
b. Comprehension
c. Application
d. Analysis

39. The famous trumpet opening in this music excerpt was composed by which of the following Romantic era composers?

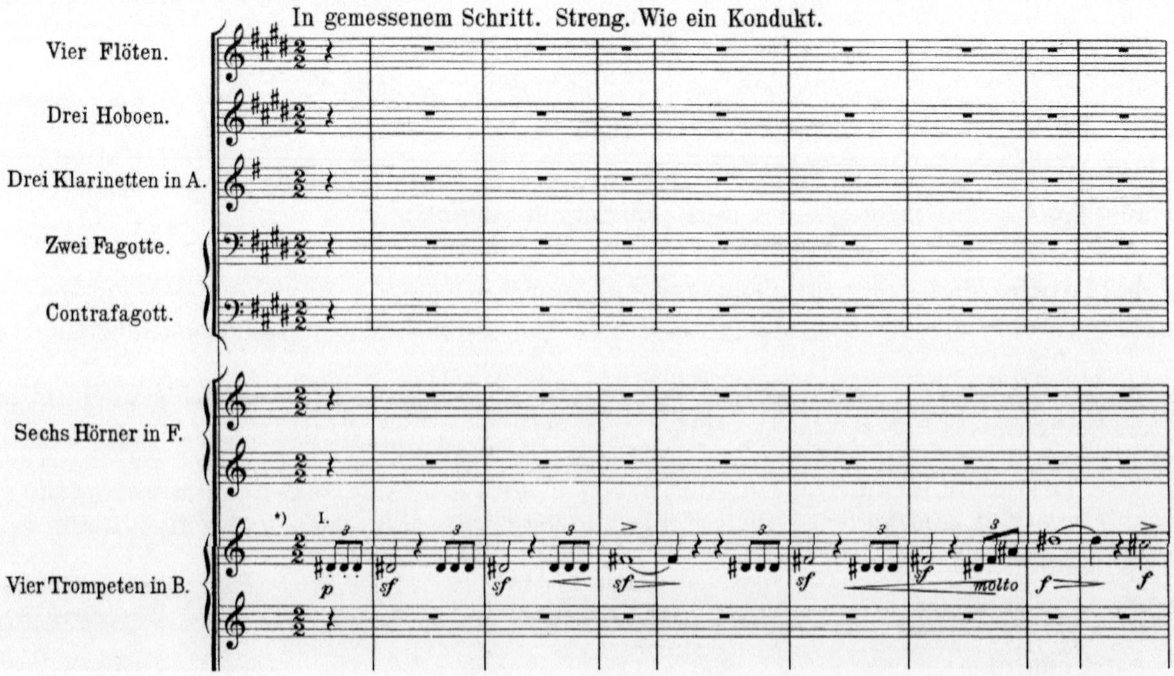

a. Mozart
b. Mahler
c. Beethoven
d. Schubert

40. Of the following, what is the best technique for using recordings in score study?

a. Listen to a variety of interpretations
b. Use recordings at every rehearsal
c. Listen to famous recordings
d. Practice conducting to the recording

41. Which of the following tonality sequences does Gordon advocate for as a part of learning sequence activities?

a. Major/minor, Dorian/Mixolydian
b. Pentatonic, major
c. Mixolydian, Dorian
d. Major/Dorian, Mixolydian/minor

42. Which of the following expenditures is a long-term budget item?

a. Repertoire purchases
b. Uniform upgrades
c. Instrument repair
d. Piano tuning

43. The Sugarhill Gang helped to widely popularize which term in their 1979 song *Rapper's Delight*?

a. Hip hop
b. Disco rap
c. Neo soul
d. Trip hop

44. Which of the following jazz standards is performed in the bossa nova style?

a. "Sweet Georgia Brown"
b. "Whispering"
c. "Stella By Starlight"
d. "The Girl from Ipanema"

45. What are the main incentives for aspiring performers to compete in local, regional, and national competitions?

a. High school and college admission
b. Performance opportunities and publicity
c. Financial and retirement stability
d. Music research and development

46. What is the name of the playing technique for French horn that produces a slightly darker tone, more easily controls pitch, and aids in performing extended techniques such as stopped horn and echo horn?

a. Left-hand technique
b. Open-fist technique
c. Hand-horn technique
d. Closed-throat technique

47. In a traditional high school music theory class, which of the following sequences of concepts from common practice period is most appropriate to teach?

a. Dominant seventh chords in root position, the III chord
b. Six-four chords, seventh chords in various inversions
c. Root position part-writing, modulations
d. Secondary dominant chords, enharmonic modulations

48. Which of the following is the most likely cause for a trumpet student's pitch to fall flat only at the ends of musical phrases?

a. Lack of breath support
b. Mouth corners being too relaxed
c. Neglecting to use the tuning slides
d. The tongue resting too high in the mouth

49. Which of the following regions of the world do raags come from?

a. Australia
b. Japan
c. Africa
d. India

50. Which of the following instructional strategies is the most practical technique to modify music instruction when teaching classical guitar in a general music classroom?

a. Separate high achievers from low achievers
b. Eliminate individual formative assessments
c. Provide each student with short personal lessons
d. Design group projects based upon mutual interests

51. When practicing with drones, which of the following techniques can be used to indicate whether one is playing in-tune with just intonation?

a. Listening for echo in the room
b. Listening for a core in the center of the tone
c. Listening for others to match pitch
d. Listening for the difference tone

52. Which of the following beginning sequences to tune a double horn is most appropriately used after completely pushing in all the slides?

a. Tune the Bb side of the horn with a tuner using a note that shares the same fingering on both sides of the horn with C5 (concert F4). Then tune the F side to the Bb side using the same note.
b. Tune the F side of the horn with a tuner using a note that it shares the same fingering on both sides with C5 (concert F4). Then tune the Bb side to the F side using the same note.
c. Tune the Bb side of the horn with a tuner using F5 (concert Bb3). Then tune the F side to a tuner using C4 (concert F4).
d. Tune both the Bb and the F sides of the horn with a tuner to E6 (concert A). Then proceed through prescribed valve combinations, starting with the first valve B4 (concert E).

53. A music teacher found guilty of willful copyright infringement for personal financial gain faces maximum penalties of which of the following?

a. A warning from the company he or she has wronged and a complaint to his or her state's licensing board
b. Two years' probation
c. Unspecified statutory damages ranging from $750 to $30,000
d. Criminal fines up to $250,000 and/or a five-year jail sentence

54. Which of the following teaches and guides improvisational skills for both instrumentalists and vocalists, specifically through audiation?

a. Irv Kratka's "Music Minus One"
b. Christopher Azzara's "Creativity in Improvisation"
c. Jamey Aebersold's "Play-Along"
d. Jerry Coker's "Patterns for Jazz"

55. For intermediate to advanced clarinet players, which pair of notes provides the most appropriate reference points for tuning a clarinet to itself?

a. G4, C5
b. E3, C5
c. E3, B4
d. B4, G4

56. Which of the following countries does the cajon come from?

a. Mexico
b. Mali
c. Peru
d. Jamaica

57. Which of the following physical actions meant to seclude a student best legally defines "physical seclusion"?

a. Involuntary confinement of a student alone in a room in which the student is physically prevented from leaving
b. A timeout, used as a behavior management technique that is part of an approved program
c. Monitored separation of a student in a non-locked setting and implemented for the purpose of calming
d. Confining a student to a locked-down area during an emergency situation, such as the presence of a school shooter

58. Which of the following composers wrote an opera based upon Shakespeare's *Othello*?

a. Verdi
b. Puccini
c. Berlioz
d. Handel

59. The black church heavily influenced which of the following musical genres through improvisation, storytelling, and call and response?

a. Metal
b. Latin
c. Grunge
d. Blues

60. Which of the following music notation copying scenarios is allowed by the 1976 Copyright Act?

a. The teacher copies one chapter from a music theory book for students.
b. The teacher makes a copy of a score to study and mark up for rehearsal.
c. The teacher copies an entire piece onto a blackboard or an interactive whiteboard.
d. The teacher simplifies a music part for a student and alters the character of the work.

61. Which of the following vocal agility considerations is among the first building blocks when learning to increase quickness and flexibility between notes in melismatic music and the music of Bach and Handel?

a. Learning to slur notes
b. Increasing tongue and jaw movement
c. Moving as quickly as possible through the scale
d. Incorporating consonants in between open vowels

62. If a vocal student is told to practice yawning, he or she most likely has the common problem of...

a. Singing with a tight throat.
b. Singing out of tune.
c. Singing with blurred words.
d. Singing without rhythm.

63. Which of the following is the most appropriate first step to tuning a student-level flute?

a. Check that the head-joint cork is in the right place using the cleaning rod's tick mark with the center of the embouchure hole.
b. Ensure that the distance from the keys to each hole is adjusted appropriately by the manufacturer.
c. Pull out the head-joint by approximately one-eighth to one-quarter of an inch and tune to a concert A.
d. Roll your flute in and out from your blowing angle to raise or lower the pitch.

64. What is the main role of the free hand when conducting an ensemble?

a. Keeping the beat
b. Musical reinforcement
c. Balance
d. Following the score

65. Which of the following musical terms most closely means that the strings are to be struck with the wood of the bow?

a. Détaché
b. Fuoco
c. Da capo
d. Col legno

66. What is the name of that range within a singer's vocal abilities that resonates in the most aesthetically pleasing manner and is usually the most comfortable to sing?

a. Chest voice
b. Tessitura
c. Falsetto
d. Register

67. Place the following brass instruments in order from brightest to darkest timbres: French horn, flugelhorn, trumpet, trombone.

a. Flugelhorn, trumpet, French horn, trombone
b. Trumpet, flugelhorn, trombone, French horn
c. Trombone, trumpet, flugelhorn, French horn
d. French horn, flugelhorn, trumpet, trombone

68. Which of the following software applications is commonly thought of as the industry standard for professional music notation?

a. MuseScore
b. GarageBand
c. Dorico
d. Cubase

69. Which major pedagogue developed the system of music education through movement called eurythmics?

a. Kodály
b. Dalcroze
c. Orff
d. Suzuki

70. What is the lower limit for a middle school male whose voice has already changed?

a. G3
b. F3
c. A3
d. D3

71. Which of the following assessment scales would be appropriate for a teacher measuring progress of her second-grade music students?

a. Letter grades, A to F
b. Percentages
c. Second graders are too young for assessments; the focus should be on an introduction to music without judgment or pressure
d. A simple system such as checks and plusses

72. Which of the following types of rating scales is illustrated?

Checklist to Measure Students' Ability to Distinguish and Sing Individual Pitches When Presented with a Major Tonic Chord
1. Student responds = 1 point
2. Sings root (*do*) = 1 point
3. Sings fifth (*so*) = 1 point
4. Sings third (*mi*) = 2 points
TOTAL POINTS = ________

a. Single-dimensional additive rating scale
b. Single-dimensional cumulative rating scale
c. Hybrid multi-dimensional additive rating scale
d. Hybrid single-dimensional cumulative rating scale

73. Which of the following tongue tension-releasing exercises best forms the basis for all exercises that help to release tension in the tongue?

a. Drinking lukewarm water to relax the tongue before vocalizing
b. Stretching the tongue using various techniques
c. Releasing tongue and jaw tension with massages and breathing exercises
d. Rolling the neck and head, keeping the mouth open and jaw down when rolling the head back

74. Which of the following textures in music is characterized by a single melodic line with instrumental accompaniment?

a. Heterophony
b. Homophony
c. Polyphony
d. Homonymy

75. Which opera form of the Enlightenment featured three acts with alternating arias and recitatives with usually six or seven characters?

a. Opera buffa
b. Opera comique
c. Opera seria
d. Opera greco

76. Which of the following is a beginning tuba player likely to have the LEAST amount of practice with in a traditional ensemble?

a. Performing melodic parts
b. Playing harmonies
c. Performing bass lines
d. Playing on time

77. Which of the following is almost always bad etiquette for a classical music performer, but not always for a member of the audience?

a. Talking during the performance
b. Leaving a cell phone on
c. Loud page turns
d. Toe tapping

78. Which of the following artifacts for a digital assessment portfolio is best suited for grade 1 general music classes?

a. A photo collage of students participating in music activities throughout the year.
b. A digital drawing of a melodic contour of a song being learned in class.
c. A digital photo of a word cloud of music terms and symbols.
d. A computer screen capture of the cycle of fourths.

79. Which of the following parent/guardian communication techniques is the best and most inclusive way to inform these stakeholders of what is happening in the music classroom?

a. Regular Blogs/Vlogs
b. Monthly parent newsletters
c. Classroom visits
d. Marking period summaries

80. What is the name of the motion of two musical lines where one line stays stationary while the other musical line moves in an upward or downward direction?

a. Contrary motion
b. Parallel motion
c. Similar motion
d. Oblique motion

Answer Key and Explanations for Test #2

1. A: Two essential rules for woodwind fingerings are:

1. Don't slide fingers

2. Don't lift fingers on one hand while pressing fingers on the other hand

Choices C and D would require lifting up a finger on the left hand while placing a finger down with the right hand, then doing the opposite after leaving the Bb. Choice B would require sliding with the fingers of the left hand.

2. C: This rationale clarifies style and form to the nearest extent possible, given that terms about genre, subgenre, form, and style are often confused and can be subjective.

Musical form describes the structure of a music composition. The following list represents common music forms:

- Strophic
- Binary
- Ternary
- Rondo
- Arch
- Sonata

There may be different styles within a particular form. For example, sonata form has developed throughout history. Sonata form developed as the first movement within the musical genre of the sonata. Sonata form was developed primarily during the Classical era, but continued to stylistically evolve throughout subsequent musical eras. For example, Beethoven's use of the sonata form is generally more complex in style, including expanding the development section, than Haydn's use of the sonata form.

3. A: If a beginner snare drum student produces a buzzing sound when playing fast, he or she is most likely hammering the drumstick onto the drum instead of allowing the drumstick to drop or bounce without tension. The snare player should grip the drumstick firmly yet in a relaxed manner so that each stroke has a flowing yet controlled movement with a full, legato sound.

4. D: Dynamics refer to how volume changes in a piece. In this excerpt, terraced dynamics are created by the sudden changing texture of the music. Figured bass is a defining characteristic of the Baroque era, but it is not used in this excerpt. Changing mood and balanced phrasing are more associated with the Classical era and not the Baroque.

5. A: Some students get easily overwhelmed if a music classroom is cluttered. Options B, C, and D are accommodations and modifications that can be made for children with special needs, but they are not specific to helping a student who might become easily overwhelmed in the music classroom. Option D may be used, in particular, when a child has occupational therapy.

6. C: Voice development will affect vocal students as the larynx enlarges and the vocal folds lengthen and thicken. The physiological changes of the vocal mechanisms tend to affect boys more than girls, evident in the "cracking" of the voice. During puberty, students will have to work towards singing voice production, pitch accuracy, and increasing vocal range.

7. D: As a general rule, pianos should be tuned between two to four times a year. This depends on the seasonal temperature and humidity changes as well as the frequency of piano use, but two to four times a year generally ensures that the piano stays maintained and in tune.

8. D: The excerpt above is Ottorino Respighi's *Fountains of Rome* – "The Triton Fountain in the Morning" ("La fontana del Tritone al mattino"). Neoclassicism is characterized by a return to aesthetics of balance and form (hence Respighi's fascination with the four sculpted fountains). Neoclassicism was a reaction against the perceived imbalance of economy and the lack of emotional restraint inherent during the Romantic era; however, compared to the Classical era, the Neoclassical era incorporated expanded instrumentation and harmonic colors.

9. A: The resting tone is *do*, and there are three flats in Eb major. The bass clef is also known as the F clef.

10. B: Many sopranos will maximize vocal tract resonance at high frequencies by creating more space in the oral cavity and relaxing the vocal tract so that the resultant sound is vibrant and sonorous. The vocal tract has optimal resonances for certain frequencies, and it is important for the singer to maximize the resonances of the vibrating vocal tract with the specific pitch frequencies.

11. B: The question and answer improvisational tool is based on dialogue structure. As in dialogue within language, there is interplay between speakers and lines: a musical line "responds" to a previous musical line, and this response can come from a different musician, instrument, group, or register within a solo performer.

12. D: When conducting, the downbeat of the pattern always indicates the strongest pulse of the pattern and is indicated by a downward stroke of the hand. The last beat of the pattern is always the weakest pulse of the pattern and is thus indicated by an upward stroke of the hand. In a 4/4 pattern then, the hand moves downward on the first beat, inward on the second beat, outward on the third beat, and upward on the fourth beat.

13. C: Arnold Schoenberg developed the twelve-tone technique of music in which all twelve pitches of the chromatic scale are treated as equal. Anton Webern, Milton Babbit, and Pierre Boulez were composers who subsequently used the twelve-tone technique in their compositions, but they did not create it.

14. D: An ostinato is defined as a short, repeating accompaniment pattern throughout a musical work that can consist of a simple rhythmic, melodic, or harmonic idea. Similar to a drone, the ostinato provides a stable foundation for the main melody line. Ostinatos are found extensively in sub-Saharan African world music, including Ethiopian music.

15. A: Polyphonic music in the West is known to have primarily begun developing with melismatic organum during the Middle Ages, in which an ornate musical line was added above plainchant. Polyphony further developed during the Renaissance. Motets during the Renaissance developed to be more imitative than Medieval motets. During the Baroque period, polyphony became extremely complex and reached its apex of popularity. Options B, C, and D are incorrect because, although each music era contains polyphonic music, polyphonic music was primarily developed and reached its peak use during the Medieval, Renaissance, and Baroque eras.

16. A: The mbira originates from Zimbabwe. The mbira is a wooden box with strips of metal attached in a way that the player can pluck them with their fingers to produce different notes. The mbira has also been used by the US band Earth, Wind & Fire.

17. D: The rhythms of music are most related to the steps taken in dance. The size of canvas in a painting would relate more to the length or orchestration of a piece, the shape of a sculpture would relate more to the structure of a musical piece, and the climax of the plot in a novel would relate more to the climax of music.

18. B: The clarinet overblows at the 12th because the barrel is cylindrical and closed at one end. Option A is incorrect because saxophones are closed but conical and overblow at the octave. Option C is incorrect because the trumpet is a closed, partly cylindrical, and partly conical instrument that overblows at the octave. Option D is incorrect because a flute is an open cylinder and overblows at the octave. In other words, the saxophone, trumpet, and flute all overblow at the octave.

19. B: The resting tone for Mixolydian is "*so*." The resting tone for Aeolian is "*la*." Characteristic harmonic functions for Mixolydian are I (*so-ti-re*) – IV (*do-mi-so*) – bVII (*fa-la-do*). Characteristic harmonic functions for Aeolian are i (*la-do-mi*) – iv (*re-fa-la*) – bVii (*so-ti-re*).

20. B: An orchestrator would most likely choose strings to represent a lush canvas of passionate sound. String instruments can sustain sound unlike percussion instruments, and with an entire section of strings, the timbre of the instruments coupled with the ease of tremolo and slide technique would easily represent a lush and passionate sound.

21. D: While all of the options may be taught to beginning students to use when practicing, students who are taught to be self-regulated in their learning evaluate their performance; identify what is needed to improve; then plan, monitor, and evaluate strategies they use to do so. Students who demonstrate self-regulated behavior are self-motivated to improve.

Option B is incorrect because breaking the music down into parts may help isolate more difficult passages to be practiced more slowly and more often, but the technique is of little use without self-monitoring. The same principle applies to breaking practice into many short sessions and establishing a routine.

22. A: The choral sound from a blocked formation tends to be better suited for homophonic pieces but can make it difficult for the singers to hear other parts. In the blocked formation, the vocal parts are solidly separated from front to back so that all sopranos are grouped at one end from front row to back row, altos are grouped next, then the tenors, and lastly the basses.

23. B: Making sure that there is a high play-to-talk ratio is relevant for both vocal and instrumental rehearsals at all grade levels. This concept ensures that students remain engaged and interested in the lessons while learning. Option A is incorrect; while it encapsulates the idea of the whole-part-whole approach to teaching, it is not a technique that should be used for every part of every rehearsal. Option C is incorrect; while sight-reading is integral to developing musicianship, it should not be considered a hard and fast rule to incorporate for every rehearsal—the needs of the moment often dictate when sight-reading can be incorporated into a rehearsal. Option D is incorrect because rehearsal pacing should generally be relatively quick. Alternating the pace between fast and slow according to the needs of the moment is a more important consideration.

24. C: Composers typically use the minor mode to convey sadness in a piece of music. The major mode is most often associated with happiness or cheerfulness, with its interval of a major third. The Mixolydian and Lydian modes sound similar to the major mode, except that the Mixolydian mode has a lowered seventh scale degree, and the Lydian mode has a raised fourth scale degree.

25. D: Sectional rehearsals allow players to fine-tune their parts together and to fix any technical or musical problems apart from the full ensemble. Sometimes, the conductor may not be aware of other hidden problems except through listening to sectional rehearsals.

26. A: Guido of Arezzo (approximately AD 991 – approximately AD 1033) used this hymn, which was written to honor John the Baptist (Paul the Deacon probably wrote the words; it is unknown if Guido composed the melody) to teach a rudimentary form of solmization (the use of solfege in reading and performing music). Each phrase begins with the six syllables that Guido used in order to help singers learn chants more quickly. By recalling the chant, a singer could recall C, D, E, F, G and A (*ut*, *re*, *mi*, *fa*, *so*, and *la*). With the exception of France, *ut* was eventually replaced with *do*. The system that arose out of the Guidonian hand technique and that is the basis for teaching in the Orff and Kodály methods today (with moveable, *la*-based minor, rather than fixed-*do*) was actually developed centuries after Guido's death. Although this hymn is significant because of solmization, Guido d'Arezzo was also instrumental in developing a three- or four-line staff in which music notation could be written, replacing neumatic notation (the excerpt above is written using modern notation). Singers no longer had to rely only on memory to sing a specific chant, as neumes did not specify pitch.

27. D: Pyotr Ilyich Tchaikovsky and Edvard Grieg. Grieg and Tchaikovsky lived and composed during the same time period, the mid- to late 19th century, and, in the case of Grieg, into the early 20th. Indeed, they met in 1888. The rest of the composers that form the answers to this question did not live during the same eras and therefore never could have met. In the case of answer A, Vivaldi died in 1741, while Chopin was not born until 1810. Answer B is incorrect, since Holst was not born until 1874, 124 years after the death of Bach. Finally, Pachelbel died in 1706, 105 years before the birth of Liszt.

28. B: Historians mark *Show Boat* (1927) by Kern and Hammerstein as the first Broadway musical with a fully integrated, serious, continuous plot. Before *Show Boat*, Broadway plays consisted of musical comedies and operettas without serious narratives. *Cats* by Andrew Lloyd Webber premiered in 1981; *Ain't Misbehavin'* by Horwitz and Maltby, Jr. premiered in 1978; and *Porgy and Bess* by George Gershwin opened in 1935.

29. D: Competitions for chair placement should be held both with advance notice and at unannounced times. Periodic competitions for first chair and so on keep more advanced students playing at their best level; many students further down the row will strive to improve their play in order to catch up. The result is a better orchestra. Therefore, answer B is incorrect; while a student's self-esteem is important, all musicians should be able to withstand the pressure of demonstrating their skills to their peers and their instructor. Accordingly, both announced and unannounced competitions have their place in this process. Daily competitions, answer A, would obviously be excessive in a student orchestra's busy schedule. Answer C, conversely, would not put *enough* motivation or pressure on the students to improve.

30. C: Vocal resonance is important for an effective vocal solo performance because it creates a well-projected sound. Singing in the proper vocal register without strain, with strong vocal cords, and with the tongue and mouth in position to maximize resonance helps to project the singing voice.

31. A: The F attachment allows a tenor trombone to play a few lower notes, but it primarily allows sixth position notes to be played in first position because it makes the instrument longer by the equivalent of five positions. Thus, instead of playing a Bb major scale with Bb = first, C = sixth, D =

fourth, etc., the scale can be played Bb = first, C = first (with trigger), D = fourth, etc. This saves a lot of movement on the slide.

32. A: While IDEA does not define least restrictive environment (LRE), the concept includes the idea that children in special education should be included with all other children whenever possible. Options B and C are incorrect; while they are included in IDEA, they are not as explicit about mainstreaming and inclusion as LRE is. Option D is incorrect because PLP is a component of an IEP that describes current, specific, and measurable information about a student's performance that is affected by a disability.

33. A: Option A is the correct answer because the ability to hear and understand the sameness and difference and then sing and move using music elements such as meter, tonality, intonation (e.g., how Western-tuned pianos perform in Hungarian minor compared to authentically tuned indigenous instruments and voices), and styles of various cultures is the basis for authentic polycultural music education. This is a strong justification for the amount of time that music teachers should spend immersing and enculturating students to polycultural music during every music class meeting. The brain rewires itself to audiate the intonation of tonalities and meters of various cultures, just as the "L" and "R"—sounds that are not in the Japanese language—must be wired into the brain of persons who are Japanese and learning to speak English. This comes about by immersing young children in the language or music and sustaining that over an extended period of time as they change their way of being. Think of how much and how long infants listen to their mother tongue before beginning to speak it. Polycultural music education must be an integral part of every music education class in order for it to be truly polycultural music education.

34. C: During a rehearsal, the director should periodically check for accurate intonation of the ensemble. Aside from beginning each rehearsal with accurate tuning, the director should isolate each different section for intonation spot checks. This teaches the students to listen attentively to themselves and also to the surrounding students.

35. C: The initial audiation range is the primary range that teachers should use when singing songs to young children, both before and while these children are first being exposed to music. Children may babble and experiment with their voices above and below this range, however, this perfect fifth was advocated by Gordon because children perceive and respond best to songs and tonal patterns within this range, enabling the music teacher to shape a young child's ability to sing in tune and expand their singing range.

36. C: Because the clarinet requires more air pressure to play (smaller aperture in the mouthpiece, smaller bore in the instrument), the embouchure must be firmer. This is accomplished by tightening the corners of the mouth.

37. A: When students choose musical instruments based upon the results of a validated timbre preference test, they are more likely to enjoy the timbre of the instrument that they choose, practice more, and stay in instrumental music programs. Option B is incorrect because there may be little relationship between the population of a recruited student's timbre preference(s) and the current instrumentation needs of a particular performing ensemble. Option C is incorrect because, while this is a true reason for using a timbre preference test, it is not as directly related to the primary reason for the use of such a test. Option D is incorrect because the timbre preference test helps gauge which timbres they prefer, and this is not related to the difficulty of the instruments.

38. A: Memorizing common practice period rules is recall of information. Option B is incorrect because comprehension is about understanding the meaning, translation, interpolation, and interpretation of instructions and problems. A student that can state a problem in their own words shows comprehension. Option C is incorrect because application is when a student uses a taught concept in a new situation, an unprompted use of an abstraction, in the classroom, or from readings during novel situations. Option D is incorrect because analysis is what happens when a student separates material or concepts into component parts so that the organizational structures may be understood (an extension of application). A student that distinguishes between facts and inferences shows analysis.

39. B: This is the famous opening ("Marche Funebre") to Mahler's *Symphony No. 5* in C# minor. Gustav Mahler (1860-1911) is probably best known for bringing the symphonic form to its apotheosis during the Romantic era. He composed nine symphonies, with *No. 5* arguably being his most famous. His late Romantic style is evidenced by the length, song-like melodic structure, complex harmony, and overall dramatic nature. His symphonies are among the most performed even to this day. The excerpt above is a standard literature for trumpeters auditioning for any major modern symphony orchestra.

40. A: When using recordings in score study, careful discretion must be made so that the conductor does not merely copy the interpretation of the recording. The conductor should listen to a variety of interpretations. The conductor should not practice conducting to the recording, should not listen only to famous recordings, and should stop listening to recordings once rehearsals have begun to be able to develop one's own interpretation.

41. A: Gordon understood that comparison by sameness and difference is the fundamental basis for all learning. Students begin with tonal patterns in major and harmonic minor tonalities not because they are inherently easier than other tonalities, but because they are the dominant tonalities in Western culture. The sequence of tonalities when using tonal patterns in learning sequence activities moves to Dorian/Mixolydian, Lydian, Phrygian, Aeolian, and Locrian while always bridging to multikeyal, multitonal, polykeyal and polytonal patterns. (Note that this does not include tunes and songs used during classroom activities—Gordon advocated using as many tonalities and meters as possible during classroom activities.) Option B is incorrect because Gordon believed that pentatonic without a clear reference to a resting tone does not promote audition—students can use any or none of the tones within pentatony as a pitch center. This does not establish an objective tonality. Thus, it does not establish a basis for sameness and difference.

42. B: Options A, C, and D are short-term expenditures. Short-term expenditures are typically defined as costs that are repeating and that take place every year. Long-term expenditures are more expensive items that require a plan to save for over a period of time. Uniform upgrades are long-term expenditures because they are large, infrequent costs.

43. A: In their 1979 hit single *Rapper's Delight*, The Sugarhill Gang helped to popularize the term "hip hop" into mainstream culture. The lyrics read: "I said a hip hop, hippie to the hippie, the hip, hip a hop, and you don't stop, a rock it to the bang bang boogie, say, up jump the boogie, to the rhythm of the boogie, the beat."

44. D: "The Girl from Ipanema" is a classic performed in the bossa nova style. While percussion instruments are integral to the samba (percussion usually outnumbers other instruments), and even though the bossa nova is derived from the samba, it can be performed even without percussion. Both the samba and bossa nova can use standard "clave rhythms," which have origins in Afro-Cuban music. The bossa nova also incorporates Brazilian rhythms into its percussion section.

In Latin music, there are two general clave rhythms, where "clave" refers to the backbone of the rhythmic structure and not the actual instrument. There is the son clave (used in samba) and the rumba clave (played with the rumba). There is also something called the bossa nova clave (Brazilian clave), however, it differs from the son clave and rumba clave in that it is not a repetitive rhythm pattern that underlies a song. It is more like a motif—one may hear it within a bossa nova, but not as explicitly (remember that a bossa nova can be played even without the use of percussion instruments).

Son clave: this pattern can be played with either measure beginning the pattern (3:2 – 2:3). This is the basic pattern for Cuban son, and it is also used in samba.

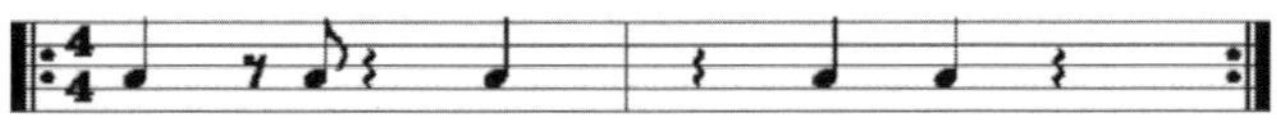

Rumba clave: this pattern can also be played with either measure beginning the pattern (3:2 – 2:3).

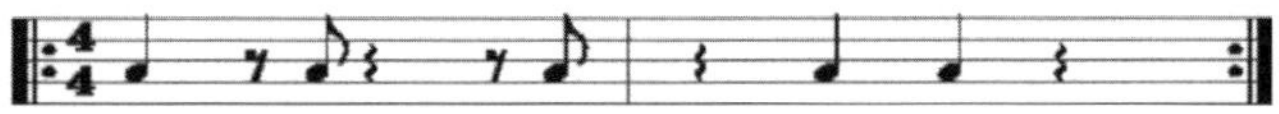

Bossa nova clave (Brazilian clave): this pattern is not a guiding pattern, but more of a rhythmic motif. Many Brazilians say that there is no clave pattern in their music and that the clave backbone is strictly Cuban.

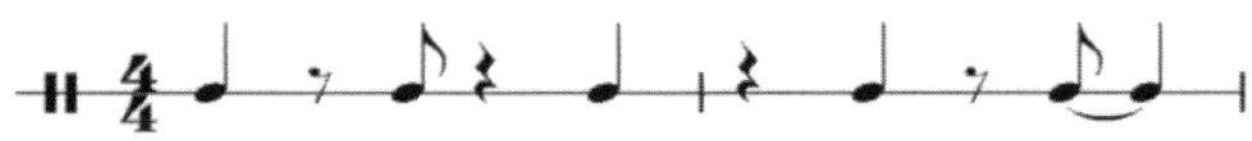

Because there are generally several percussion instruments in Latin music, there are other rhythm patterns that are imposed on these basic guiding patterns. Melodic instruments can also play additional repeated rhythm patterns under or over these basic claves and the bossa nova motif, making a polyrhythmic performance.

(Note: The late George Michael song, "Faith" (1987), contains a 3:2 son clave in the rhythm guitar. Santana's "Oye Como Va" (1970) contains another example of a son clave.)

45. B: The main incentives for aspiring performers to compete in local, regional, and national competitions are performance opportunities and publicity. As an aspiring performer, the additional performances and publicity gained from placing in competitions will help with college admissions, which in turn will help with long-term career and financial goals.

46. C: Hand-horn technique, also known as right hand technique, is the placement of the right hand inside the bell of the horn to produce a slightly darker tone, to more easily control pitch, and to perform extended techniques such as stopped horn and echo horn.

47. C: Option C is correct because root position part-writing provides a readiness to learn about modulations. Options A, B, and D are incorrect because they are backwards in sequence. Each concept is designed to provide readiness for the next concept and/or taught along with the evolution of practices over time, and is designed to promote a deeper understanding of common practice period standards.

48. A: The most likely cause for a trumpet student's pitch to fall flat only at the ends of musical phrases is a lack of proper breath support. Without a steady stream of air supported by the diaphragm and proper embouchure, the tendency is for pitches to fall flat only at the ends of musical phrases when the student runs out of breath.

49. D: "Raag" is another word for raga, Indian music with a melodic framework for musicians to improvise in. In American music, major and minor tonalities predominate the culture. But India has over 300 ragas, meaning "color." Just as each color is unique, each raga has a distinct sound. A raga melody is sung or played on a sitar and can be accompanied by percussion instruments, such as the tabla.

50. D: Option D is the correct answer because teachers can group by student preferences when offering choices of tunes or songs that students want to learn, learning about the history and use of the guitar in different cultural settings or genres, and then having the different groups of students present their findings and perform to the rest of the class, etc. Option A is incorrect because high and low achievers learn from one another (often more than they do from the teacher), even when differentiating instruction, such as progressing with tonal and rhythm patterns through Gordon's skill learning sequence, or when assigning students different tunes or songs to learn as homework in order to play for the class, etc. Option B is incorrect because formative assessment assists the teacher in deciding how to differentiate instruction based upon achievement and preferences. Option C is incorrect because it is impractical to provide individual lessons to each student. A better option is to pair high achievers with low achievers for peer coaching.

51. D: The difference tone (also known as the Tartini tone) sounds *in the ear* below two tones that are being played together with sustain and intensity. Tartini advocated listening for the difference tone when playing double stops on a stringed instrument in order to achieve good, beatless intonation. Option A is incorrect because room echo does not indicate intonation. Option B is incorrect because a core sound in the center of the tone indicates a developed embouchure and performing in synchrony with the pitch tendencies of a particular instrument, but the core tone does not indicate that one is performing beatless harmonies with a drone. Option C is incorrect because drones are used primarily in individual practice sessions in order for an individual to learn to perform with various temperaments; however, a second player can sometimes perform the drone.

52. A: The Bb side is the side that the F side is compared to, thus the Bb side is tuned first. The instrument is tuned on the Bb side to a C5 (concert F) because the horn, no matter which side is being played, is considered a horn in F, and the notation and fingerings for the concert F for each side is the same (open fingering).

After this step, one may proceed to tune each valve through a prescribed sequence of valve combinations, starting with the first valve. Note that tuning a double horn is always a compromise, and a well-developed embouchure and slight pushing in or pulling out of the hand in the bell can raise or lower the pitch.

When tuning a horn for a younger student, when tuning all of the valves, one can mark all the slides with a pencil in order to save time tuning a section the next time around.

53. D: The teacher could face criminal fines up to $250,000 and/or a five-year sentence. The penalties are extremely severe for educators who photocopy music or commit other copyright infringement for personal monetary gain. Copyright law is strict, even in an age music content and sheet music often appears free for the taking. While companies are given the discretion to warn teachers in writing, they do have the option of pursuing more severe penalties. Therefore, answer A is incorrect. Both two years' probation and the unspecified statutory damages of $750 to $30,000 are incorrect, as they do not refer to the maximum penalty a teacher can face if he or she chooses to violate copyright protection for personal gain.

54. B: Christopher Azzara's "Creativity in Improvisation" series focuses on audiation-based techniques to help students improve their improvisational skills. "Music Minus One" is similar to karaoke in that a student performs the missing part on a recording. "Play-Along" encourages the memorization, experimentation, and application of scales along with recorded tunes as one teaches him or herself to improvise through aleatory experience. "Patterns for Jazz" is a popular book with patterns that a musician transposes to different keys and uses while learning to improvise through experimentation and self-teaching.

55. A: When tuning a clarinet to itself, players check intonation by comparing reference tones. The notes G4 and C5 are often used as reference tones because they represent different registers and adjustment points on the instrument. The open throat tone G4 has no fingers down, thus presenting the entire open length of the clarinet. Clarion C5 is played using both the left hand and the right hand, and the adjustment is made with the middle joint.

56. C: The cajon is a wooden box percussion instrument. Peruvian slaves from West Africa created it using packing crates to replace the percussion instruments that they left behind. Western pop music has adopted the use of the cajon. Drummers can now be seen performing pop songs while sitting on a cajon and beating Western rhythm to pop music.

57. A: The involuntary confinement of a student alone in a room in which the student is physical prevented from leaving best legally defines "physical seclusion." The difference between option A and option D should be self-evident, as emergency situations require such tactics for student safety; however, the US Department for Civil Rights has yet to address the issue of option D in its manual. Option B is incorrect because it is part of a sanctioned behavior modification program. Option C is incorrect because it is an extension of option B and is part of a timeout. The US Department Office for Civil Rights explains that restraint or seclusion should never be used as "punishment or discipline... as a means of coercion or retaliation, or as a convenience" (p.12).

58. A: Verdi's opera *Otello* premiered in 1887 and was based on Shakespeare's *Othello*. It was Verdi's second-to-last opera. Gioachino Rossini also wrote a well-known opera called *Otello*, but his version was not based on Shakespeare's *Othello*.

59. D: Blues music was heavily influenced by the black church through improvisation, storytelling, call and response, vocal inflections, and the blues progression. Many of these musical features are now representative of the blues genre of music.

60. C: Under the 1976 Copyright Act, teachers are allowed to copy an entire piece onto a board in a classroom. Option A is incorrect because a teacher may make only one copy of one chapter from a book for scholarly research or teacher preparation. Option B is incorrect because copyright law does not allow an entire music score to be copied. Option D is incorrect because the fundamental character of the work is altered, which is prohibited by copyright law.

61. D: Starting with an "N" consonant before the vowel keeps the voice forward in the mouth and helps to separate the notes, as agility involves smoothness and legato without slurring in between notes. Once a legato style is achieved with adequate abdominal support that does not produce tension at a slower tempo and then a faster tempo, the consonants can be removed. Option B is incorrect because there should be economy of tongue and jaw movement when performing passages that require agile vocalization. Option C is incorrect because learning vocal agility starts with exercises that are relatively slower in tempo.

62. A: If a vocal student is told to practice yawning, he or she most likely has the common problem of singing with a tight throat. The yawn helps the throat to achieve its most open and relaxed state, necessary for productive and healthy singing.

63. A: Option B is incorrect because key height is usually checked for leaks in the tone holes and for appropriate venting. For example, if a key is too low, it creates a stuffy sound by blocking the air flow out of the key hole. Adjusting key height is also used to correct intonation problems on one or several keys on the flute; however, it is generally not a first step in tuning a flute, as manufacturer specifications are generally close to the correct height. Flute players often wish to lower the distance between the key and keyhole to increase speed and dexterity.

Option C is incorrect because adjusting the head-joint is done after ensuring that the head-joint cork is in the correct position. Further, concert D5 is often used, particularly for beginning and intermediate students, because the note is not very bendable and both hands are balanced on the flute. Option D is incorrect because changing the angle to raise or lower a pitch is done only as a fine-tuning technique, primarily to account for individual pitch tendencies on a particular flute, as tone problems can become an issue when rolling the flute. The best initial step is to check that the head-joint cork is in the right place with the cleaning rod, as this ensures that the flute's internal tuning is set.

64. B: The main role of the free hand when conducting an ensemble is as musical reinforcement. As an independent stimulus, the free hand can reinforce dynamics such as crescendos and decrescendos as well as aid in cueing parts. The free hand should also indicate releases, phrasing, musical style, and necessary modifications in the balance of the ensemble.

65. D: *Col legno* means to strike the strings with the wood of the bow, which matches the question stem. *Détaché* means to play the notes separately. *Fuoco* means to play in a fiery manner. *Da capo* means "from the head" (beginning).

66. B: Tessitura refers to that range within a singer's vocal abilities that resonates in the most aesthetically pleasing manner and that is generally the most comfortable for the singer. Tessitura differs from vocal range in that the range of a singer's voice refers to the limits of pitches the singer is able to sing.

67. B: These are the brass instruments given in order from brightest to darkest timbres: trumpet, flugelhorn, trombone, and French horn. The size and aspect of the conical bore affects the instrument's timbre, and of the four instruments, trumpets have the narrowest and most cylindrical bore, while the French horn has the widest and biggest bore.

68. C: Options B and D are very popular digital audio workstations, and Option A is a popular open-source desktop music publishing application, but it is not as sophisticated as Dorico and is not the industry standard for professional music writing notation software. Ultimately, the difference in effectiveness may be dictated by features that are accessible, such as MIDI input functionality. Usually, paid software comes with more support and stronger features within the platform, however, students and teachers have access to satisfactory features through free-to-use software. For many years, *Finale* was the industry standard, but it is no longer available for sale as of 2024. Dorico has since taken a leading role in the professional space as Finale has declined.

69. B: The system of music education through movement called eurythmics was developed around 1900 by Swiss composer, musician, and pedagogue Émile Jaques-Dalcroze, in which students use a kinesthetic approach to experience musical concepts. The body is seen as the instrument, and students discover musicality, tempo, dynamics, and phrase structure through physical dialogue with the music.

70. D: The lower limit for a middle school male whose voice has already changed is D3. Although the voice has changed, it is still developing and will not have the range—or the strength and endurance—of a choral high school tenor or bass.

71. D: A simple system such as checks (for meeting the standard) and plusses (for exceeding them). A third symbol, such as an O for approaching the standard, also would be appropriate. Answer A, assigning letter grades, would be appropriate only for older students, and then only as an overall grade. Therefore, (A) is incorrect. Also incorrect is (B), percentages, since they would be overly detailed and unnecessary to assess the basic process of students so young. Conversely, (C), which asserts that second graders are too young for assessment, is incorrect, as state and national standards exist for students as young as those of pre-school age.

72. D: Option D is the correct answer because students are being measured on one dimension; however, while it is objectively unknown whether the tonic or the fifth is easier to distinguish and sing (e.g., many students with low music aptitude often sing the fifth), it is clear that distinguishing and singing the third is more difficult. An additive scale has multiple questions that are independently graded, whereas a cumulative scale has interrelated items. Since this checklist has independent scoreable items, it is an additive scale.

73. B: Tongue stretching exercises include sticking out the tongue in various directions as far as possible, then relaxing; yawning while producing a soft-sounding siren, which allows the tongue to come out and down; stretching the tongue out and down to produce a circle of sound that cannot be broken if the tongue is relaxed; and placing the tip of the tongue at the bottom of the front teeth and arching the tongue forward so that the back of the tongue can be felt (this exercise can also be done when placing a curl within the tongue while phonating). Options A, C, and D are all other techniques to improve vocalization by relaxing the tongue, but tongue stretches are paramount.

74. B: Homophonic music can have accompaniment that is in the style of block chords, or the accompaniment may have some subjective polyphonic characteristics, such as a guitar accompaniment in pop music in which the performer picks instead of strums. It can also have an accompaniment in which there are harmonic layers. Option A is incorrect because heterophony involves variations of a melodic line played simultaneously. Option C is incorrect because polyphony involves multiple independent melodic lines. Option D is incorrect because it refers to word meaning—lexical semantics—in language. Homonymy refers to words that have the same sound (homophones) or orthographic form

75. C: The *opera seria* that arose during the Enlightenment focused on tragic and serious subjects. The structure, number of singers, and plot line were structured so that the action usually took place in three acts with alternating arias and recitatives, and the number of characters usually numbered six or seven with two to four main characters.

76. A: All tuba students should have competencies related to comprehensive musicianship. A challenge for tuba players at all levels of development is the limited nature of their ensemble parts. Tuba parts in ensemble pieces tend to be harmonies or bass lines. This can lead to a lack of practice playing melodic lines. Incorporating more melodic practice can make tuba players more comprehensive musicians. Edwin Gordon and Richard Grunow's *Jump Right In: The Instrumental Series* and Christopher Azzara's *Creativity in Improvisation* series accommodates tuba and other low brass players, affording students the opportunity to become comprehensive musicians.

77. D: Student performers should move to the music and can gently sway during classical concerts, but toe tapping is always distracting to at least some of the audience. An audience member may quietly tap a toe if it is not distracting to others. One might think that option C pertains only to the performer, but many persons who attend concerts bring books and magazines.

78. B: There are three general types of portfolios, each with distinct purposes, but also overlapping in some areas. These are the working portfolio, the display portfolio, and the assessment portfolio. Option B is correct because it is appropriate for an assessment-type portfolio and is grade appropriate. Option A is incorrect because, while it is part of a digital portfolio and is more suitable to a display-type portfolio. Options C and D are incorrect because, while they are both part of a digital portfolio, they are not age appropriate.

79. A: While invitations to parents to visit the classroom on a regular basis are important opportunities for parents to see what is happening in the music program, many parents cannot take time out of their day to regularly come to visit the classroom. Emailing blogs with videos of students engaged in classroom activities allows parents and other stakeholders to see and hear what is happening in the classroom when they do not have the time to physically attend classes. Weekly newsletters and marking period summaries are also important tools for communicating and gaining stakeholder buy-in, but are not as personal, informative or complete as regular blogging/vlogging.

80. D: Oblique motion refers to the motion of two musical lines in which one line stays stationary while the other musical line moves in an upward or downward direction. Contrary motion moves in opposite directions, parallel motion moves in the same direction, and similar motion refers to the motion of two musical lines that move in similar directions.